Zaner-Bloser
Handwriting
With continuous-stroke alphabet

Author

Clinton S. Hackney

Contributing Authors

Pamela J. Farris
Janice T. Jones
Linda Leonard Lamme

Zaner-Bloser, Inc., P.O. Box 16764, Columbus, Ohio 43216-6764   1-800-421-3018

D1318665

Copyright © 1999 Zaner-Bloser, Inc.   ISBN 0-88085-955-5

Developed by Kirchoff/Wohlberg, Inc., in cooperation with Zaner-Bloser Publishers

Printed in the United States of America

98 99 00 01 02 WC 5 4 3 2 1

You already know handwriting is important.
Now take a look at...

NEW SIMPLIFIED

Zaner-Bloser Handwriting

Easier to read!   Easier to write!   Easier to teach!

Zaner-Bloser's new
program is easy to teach.

I see Zaner-Bloser's
alphabet in the books I read.

I like Zaner-Bloser because
it's so easy to write.

You already know handwriting is important, but did you know...

Did You Know...

Annually, the U.S. Postal Service receives 38 million illegibly addressed letters, costing American taxpayers $4 million each year.

–American Demographics, Dec. 1992

Did You Know...

Hundreds of thousands of tax returns are delayed every year because figures, notes, and signatures are illegible.

–Better Handwriting in 30 Days, 1989

Did You Know...

Poor handwriting costs American business $200 million annually.

–American Demographics, Dec. 1992

Zaner-Bloser's CONTINUOUS-STROKE manuscript alphabet

Aa Bb Cc Dd Ee Ff Gg
Oo Pp Qq Rr Ss Tt

Easier to Read

Our vertical manuscript alphabet is like the alphabet kids see every day inside and outside of the classroom. They see it in their school books, in important environmental print like road signs, and in books and cartoons they read for fun.

"[Slanted] manuscript is not only harder to learn than traditional [vertical] print, but it creates substantially more letter recognition errors and causes more letter confusion than does the traditional style."

–Debby Kuhl and Peter Dewitz in a paper presented at the 1994 meeting of the American Educational Research Association

Please, my friends, a moment of silence, as the flying Zucchinis attempt a twisting triple somersault.

CALIFORNIA LIN 216

STOP

Vertical manuscript is the alphabet we see every day.

CIRCUS by Lois Ehlert ©1992 by Lois Ehlert

iv

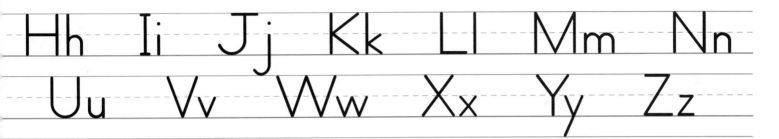

Easier to Write

Our vertical manuscript alphabet is written with continuous strokes—fewer pencil lifts—so there's a greater sense of flow in writing. And kids can write every letter once they learn four simple strokes that even kindergartners can manage.

Four simple strokes: circle, horizontal line, vertical line, slanted line

"The writing hand has to change direction more often when writing the [slanted] alphabet, do more retracing of lines, and make more strokes that occur later in children's development."

–Steve Graham in *Focus on Exceptional Children*, 1992

Many kids can already write their names when they start school (vertical manuscript).

Kirk

Why should they have to relearn them in another form (slanted manuscript)? With Zaner-Bloser, they don't have to.

Kirk

Easier to Teach

Our vertical manuscript alphabet is easy to teach because there's no reteaching involved. Children are already familiar with our letterforms—they've seen them in their environment and they've learned them at home.

"Before starting school, many children learn how to write traditional [vertical] manuscript letters from their parents or preschool teachers. Learning a special alphabet such as [slanted] means that these children will have to relearn many of the letters they can already write."

–Steve Graham in *Focus on Exceptional Children*, 1992

Zaner-Bloser's NEW SIMPLIFIED cursive alphabet

Aa Bb Cc Dd Ee Ff Gg

Nn Oo Pp Qq Rr Ss

Simplified letterforms...
Easier to read and write

old letterform

Letterforms are simplified so they're easier to write and easier to identify in writing. The new simplified **Q** now looks like a **Q** instead of a number 2.

old letterform

Our simplified letterforms use the headline, midline, and baseline as a guide for where letters start and stop. The new simplified **d** touches the headline instead of stopping halfway.

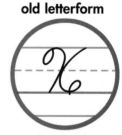

old letterform

No more "cane stems!" Our new simplified letterforms begin with a small curve instead of fancy loops that can be difficult for students to write.

Hh Ii Jj Kk Ll Mm

Tt Uu Vv Ww Xx Yy Zz

Simplified letterforms...
Easier to teach

When handwriting is easy for students to write, instruction time is cut way back! That's the teaching advantage with Zaner-Bloser Handwriting. Our cursive letterforms are simplified so instead of spending a lot of time teaching fancy loops that give kids trouble, teachers give instruction for simple, basic handwriting that students can use for the rest of their lives.

And remember, with Zaner-Bloser Handwriting, students learn to write manuscript with continuous strokes. That means that when it's time for those students to begin writing cursive, the transition comes naturally because they already know the flow of continuous strokes.

These simple letters are so much easier to teach!

The Student Edition...a child-centered text

Uppercase and lowercase letterforms are taught together.

Children write letters first, then words, and finally complete sentences.

Children trace models first before writing on their own.

Writing practice is done directly beneath a model that is easy for both right- and left-handers to see.

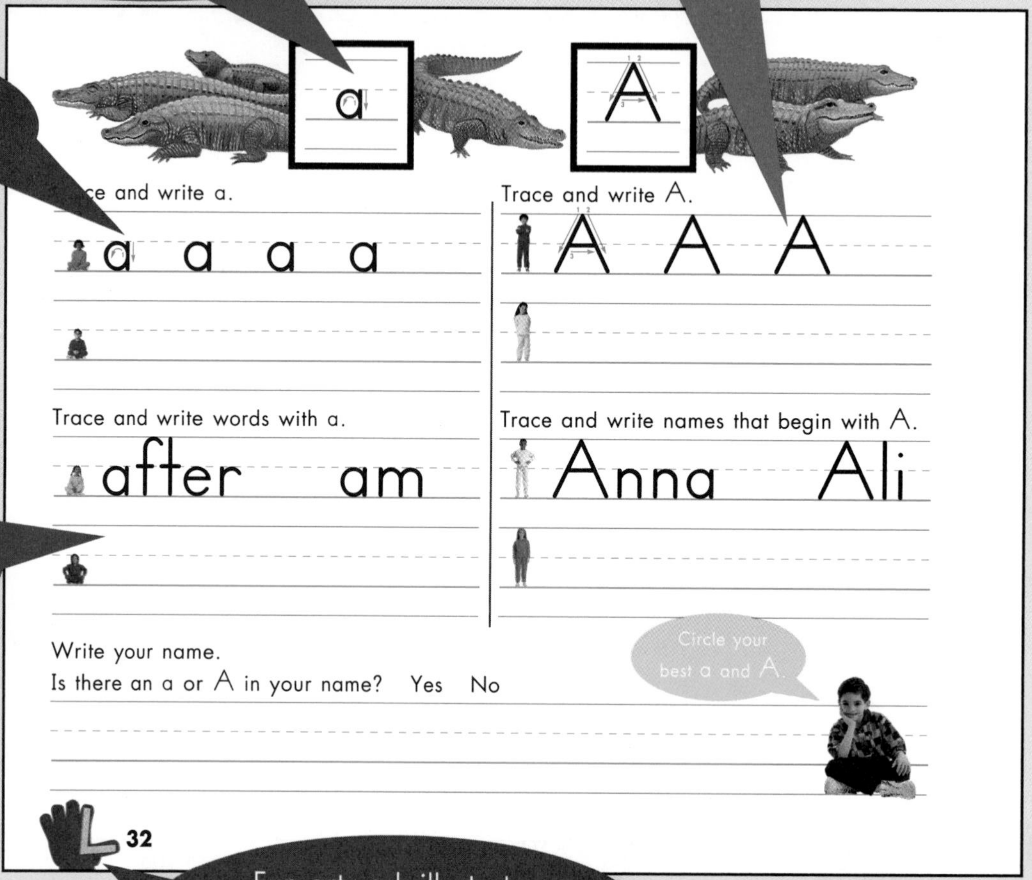

Trace and write a.

a a a a a

Trace and write A.

A A A A

Trace and write words with a.

after   am

Trace and write names that begin with A.

Anna   Ali

Write your name.
Is there an a or A in your name?   Yes   No

Circle your best a and A.

32

Fun artwork illustrates concepts like *left* and *right*.

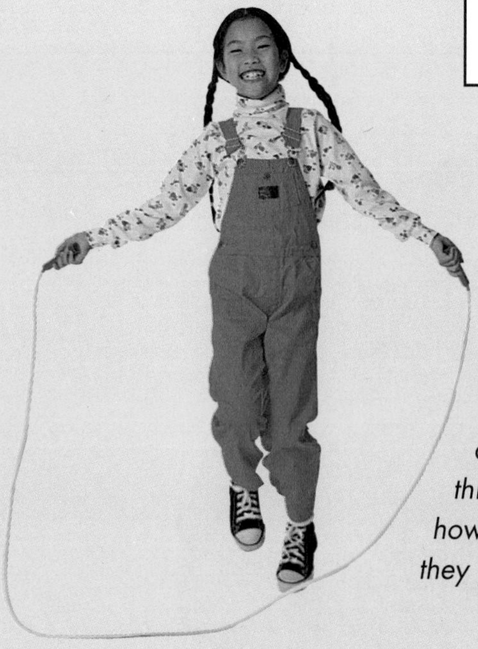

Language arts connections are easy with activities like this one. Here, children learn how to make contractions as they practice their handwriting.

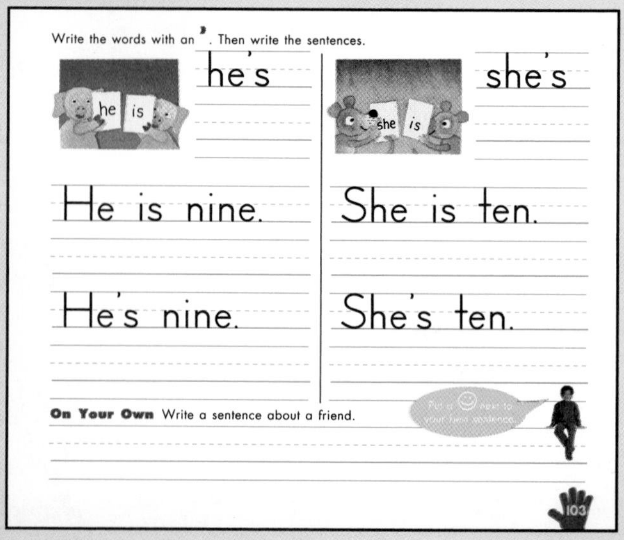

Write the words with an ' . Then write the sentences.

he is   he's   she is   she's

He is nine.   She is ten.

He's nine.   She's ten.

On Your Own Write a sentence about a friend.

Put a ☺ near to your best sentence.

103

Realistic illustrations of animals connect letters and sounds.

Letter models with arrows show stroke direction and sequence.

Child-like art is fun and motivating.

Children evaluate their own handwriting on every page.

Personal writing activities help make language arts connections.

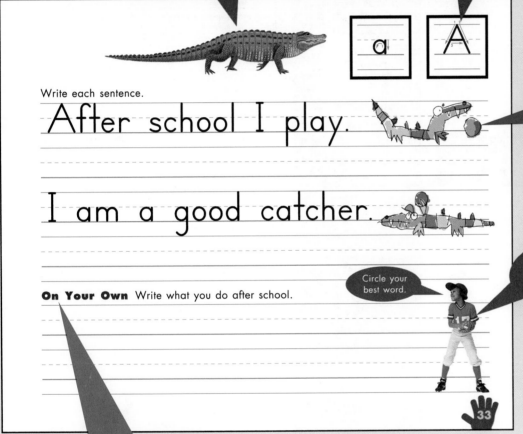

Write each sentence.

After school I play.

I am a good catcher.

On Your Own Write what you do after school.

Circle your best word.

33

Grade I Student Edition

Children learn to appreciate diverse cultures through activities like this one, in which they write "hello" in four different languages.

Hola Means Hello Write **hello** in four languages.

English
Hello!

French
Bonjour!

Spanish
¡Hola!

Swahili
Jambo!

On Your Own Write what you say when you answer the phone.

Circle your best word.

106

The Teacher Edition...streamlined instruction

At-a-glance stroke descriptions are short and easy to find.

Brief teaching notes save you valuable time.

Corrective strategies offer solutions to common handwriting problems.

CONTINUOUS STROKE

Touch below the midline; circle back (left) all the way around. Push up straight to the midline. Pull down straight to the baseline.

Touch the headline; slant left to the baseline. Lift. Touch the headline; slant right to the baseline. Lift. Touch the midline; slide right.

MODEL
Write **a** on guidelines as you say the stroke descriptions. Model writing **a** in the air as you repeat the descriptions. Have children echo them as they write **a** in the air with you. Follow the same procedure for **A**.

PRACTICE
Let children practice writing **a** and **A** on laminated writing cards or slates before they write on the pages.

32

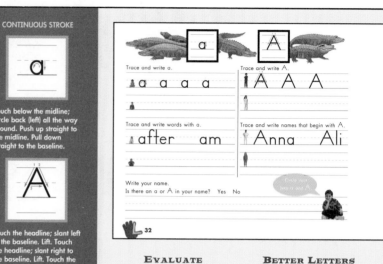

Trace and write a.

a a a a

Trace and write A.

A A A

Trace and write words with a.

after   am

Trace and write names that begin with A.

Anna   Ali

Write your name.
Is there an a or A in your name?   Yes   No

32

EVALUATE

a a a

To help children evaluate their writing, ask questions such as these:
Is your circle round?
Does your **a** touch the midline?

A A A

Are your strokes straight?
Is your slide right stroke on the midline?
Do your slant strokes touch the headline at the same spot?
Is your **A** about the same width as the model?

BETTER LETTERS

O   a

To help children write **a** without lifting the pencil, remind them not to lift the pencil from the paper after the circle back stroke but to go right into the push up stroke. Put three aligned dots as shown and refer to them as you give the stroke descriptions.

A   A

To help children write **A** the correct width, place two dots on the baseline and a dot on the headline as shown. Have them connect the dots with slant left and slant right lines and make a slide right line on the midline.

Grade I Teacher Edition

x

Write each sentence.

After school I play.

I am a good catcher.

On Your Own Write what you do after school.

Circle your best word.

33

FUN and GAMES
WRITING CORNER

Record letter names and stroke descriptions on an audiocassette tape. Use these letters: A, a, O, o, T, t, I, i, L, l. Provide a cassette player. Invite children to listen and write the letters following the descriptions on the tape. Make new cassette tapes as other letters are introduced. Later, make a game of the procedure by describing a letter for children to write in the air. Have them call out the letter as they recognize it. (auditory, kinesthetic)

PHONICS CONNECTION

Prepare a tray of wet sand or shaving cream on a table. Tell children to listen for words that begin with the first sound they hear in *alligator*. Then say words such as *ask, apple, dog, tree,* and *ax.* Tell children to write **a** in the sand or shaving cream if the word begins like *alligator.* Repeat with names of people and have children write **A.** (auditory, kinesthetic)

WRITE SENTENCES

Before children write the two sentences on the page, write the word *school* three ways: correctly spaced, spaced too far apart, and spaced too close together. Have them comment on the spacing in each word. After children write, have them work in pairs to comment on the spacing of letters in words their partners have written. Guide children to recognize why one word might be better than another.

COACHING HINT

Children need to develop a clear mental image of the letter to be written. They should look at the letter first. To help them develop such an image, ask questions about the shape and size of the letter and the kinds of strokes used to form it. For A, children should note the slant lines and may form them by holding their two index fingers together in a slant. (visual)

PRACTICE MASTER 27

Trace and write.

a a a a a a a a

all are ask ant any

Write your own words.

Name

Copyright © Zaner-Bloser, Inc.   PRACTICE MASTER 27

PRACTICE MASTER 28

Trace and write.

A A A A A

Arnie ate the apples

Write a name that begins with A.

Name

Copyright © Zaner-Bloser, Inc.   PRACTICE MASTER 28

33

Grade 1 Teacher Edition

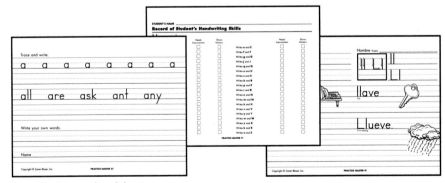

Grade 1 Practice Masters

An accompanying book of practice masters offers additional practice for every letter and skill children learn. It also includes resources to make teaching easier—certificates, an evaluation record, letters to send home to keep parents and guardians involved, and Spanish activities.

Evaluation and Assessment... consistent guidance throughout the year

Student self-evaluation...

In every lesson. Children evaluate their own handwriting and circle their best work.

In every review. Five times a year, children review the letterforms they've learned and again evaluate their handwriting.

In every evaluation. Three times each year, children "show what they can do" in an evaluation lesson. After writing words and stories, they again evaluate their handwriting.

Teacher assessment...

In every lesson and review. As children evaluate their own writing, teachers can assess their letterforms, as well as their comprehension of good handwriting. A Better Letters section for each lesson offers teachers helpful hints for common handwriting problems.

In every evaluation. Children's creative writing and drawings offer lots of opportunity for informal assessment of handwriting, language arts, and other areas.

The Keys to Legibility

These four Keys to Legibility are taught and reviewed throughout the program.
They remind children that their goal should be legible handwriting.

Size

Consistently sized letters are easy to read. Children learn to use midlines and headlines to guide the size of their letters.

Slant

Vertical letters are easier to read. Children learn how to position their papers and hold their pencils so writing vertical letters comes with ease.

Shape

Four simple strokes—circle, horizontal line, vertical line, and slanted line—make it easy for children to write letters with consistent and proper shape.

Spacing

Correct spacing between letters and words makes handwriting easy to read. Practical hints show children how to determine correct spacing.

I can draw a picture.

I can write a story about my picture.

One day I went on a long trip. I went to Mexico. I saw a liz...

Put a 😊 next to your best sentence.

Creative writing in each evaluation lesson allows the teacher to informally assess handwriting and language skills.

Completed Grade 1 Student Edition

Evaluation
Show What You Can Do
Here are words I can write.

run   ran
map   mat
van   very
kite   play
box   fox
fine   good

Write your name.
Terry Lee

90

bus   play
run   map

van   hurry
kite   yellow
box   zoo

Circle your best word.

In every evaluation lesson, students evaluate their own handwriting.

A huge collection of supplementary materials... makes handwriting even easier to teach!

A **Evaluation Guides** *grades 1–6*

B **Poster/Wall Chart Super Pak**
grades K–6, includes Handwriting Positions
Wall Chart, Keys to Legibility Wall Chart,
Alphabet Wall Chart, Simplified Stroke
Descriptions, and a Portfolio Assessment Guide

C **Story Journals** *grades K–4*

D **Manuscript/Cursive Card Set** *grades 1–6*

E **Sentence Strips** *grades K–6*

F **Writing Journals** *grades 1–6*

G **My ABC Journal** *grades K–1*

H **Pignic Alphabet Book** *grades K–2*

I **From Anne to Zach Alphabet Book** *grades K–2*

J **Letter Cards** *grades K–2*

K **Manuscript/Cursive Fonts**

L **Manuscript Kin-Tac Cards** *grades K–2*

For more information about these materials, call 1-800-421-3018.

M **Make-Your-Own Big Book** *grades K–2*

N **Parent Brochures** *for manuscript/cursive*

O **Book of Transparencies** *grades 1–6*

P **Read, Write, and Color Alphabet Mat** *grades K–2*

Q **Dry Erase Write-On Cards** *grades K–2*

R **Parent/Student Worksheets** *grades 2–6*

S **Peek Thrus** *grades 1–4*

T **Illustrated Alphabet Strips** *grades K–4*

U **Desk Strips** *grades 1–6*

V **Practice Masters** *grades K–6*

W **Alphabet Wall Strips** *grades K–6*

X **Fun With Handwriting** *grades K–8*

Y **Write-On, Wipe-Off Magnetic Board With Letters** *grades K–2*

Z **Post Office Kit** *grades K–4*

Vertical vs. *Slanted Manuscript*

What the research shows

Using a slanted alphabet has been a trend in handwriting instruction. It's actually not a new development—the first slanted alphabet was created in 1968. A sort of bridge between manuscript and cursive, this slanted alphabet used unconnected letterforms like the traditional vertical manuscript, but its letterforms were slanted like cursive.

It seemed like a good idea. This alphabet was to be easier to write than cursive, yet similar enough to cursive that children wouldn't learn two *completely* different alphabets. But after several years of use in some schools, research has uncovered some unfortunate findings.

Slanted manuscript can be difficult to write

Slanted manuscript was created to be similar to cursive, so it uses more complicated strokes such as small curves, and these strokes can be difficult for young children.

Vertical manuscript, on the other hand, is consistent with the development of young children. Each of its letters is formed with simple strokes—straight lines, circles, and slanted lines. One researcher found that the strokes used in vertical manuscript are the same as the shapes children use in their drawings (Farris, 1993). Because children are familiar with these shapes, they can identify and form the strokes with little difficulty.

Slanted manuscript can create problems with legibility

Legibility is an important goal in handwriting. Obviously, content should not be sacrificed for legibility, but what is handwriting if it cannot be read?

Educational researchers have tested the legibility of slanted manuscript and found that children writing vertical manuscript "performed significantly better" than those writing slanted manuscript. The writers of the slanted alphabet tended to make more misshapen letterforms, tended to extend their strokes above and below the guidelines, and had a difficult time keeping their letterforms consistent in size (Graham, 1992).

On the other hand, the vertical manuscript style of print has a lot of support in the area of research. Advertisers have known for years that italic type has a lower readability rate than vertical "roman" type. Research shows that in 30 minute readings, the italic style is read 4.9% slower than roman type (14–16 words per minute). This is why most literature, especially literature for early readers, is published using roman type.

Slanted manuscript can impair letter recognition

Educators have suspected that it would be beneficial for students to write and read the same style of alphabet. In other words, if children *read* vertical manuscript, they should also *write* vertical manuscript. Now it has been found that inconsistent alphabets may actually be detrimental to children's learning.

Researchers have found that slanted manuscript impairs the ability of some young children to recognize many letters. Some children who learn the slanted style alphabet find it difficult to recognize many of the traditional letterforms they see in books and environmental print. "[These children] consistently had difficulty identifying several letters, often making the same erroneous response to the same letter," the researchers reported. They concluded that slanted manuscript "creates substantially more letter recognition errors and causes more letter confusion than does the traditional style." (Kuhl & Dewitz, 1994).

Slanted manuscript does not help with transition

One of the benefits proposed by the creators of the slanted manuscript alphabet was that it made it easier for children to make the transition from manuscript to cursive writing. However, no difference in transition time has been found between the two styles of manuscript alphabets. In addition, the slanted style does not seem to enhance young children's production of cursive letters (Graham, 1992).

The slanted style of manuscript appeared to be a good idea. But educators should take a close look at what the research shows before adopting this style of alphabet. As one researcher has said, "Given the lack of supportive evidence and the practical problems involved in implementation, slanted manuscript letters cannot be recommended as a replacement for the traditional manuscript alphabet" (Graham, 1994).

> *"...slanted manuscript letters cannot be recommended as a replacement for the traditional manuscript alphabet."*

Farris, P.J. (1993). Learning to write the ABC's: A comparison of D'Nealian and Zaner-Bloser handwriting styles. *Indiana Reading Quarterly, 25* (4), 26–33.

Graham, S. (1992). Issues in handwriting instruction. *Focus on Exceptional Children, 25* (2).

Graham, S. (1994, Winter). Are slanted manuscript alphabets superior to the traditional manuscript alphabet? *Childhood Education,* 91–95.

Kuhl, D. & Dewitz, P. (1994, April). The effect of handwriting style on alphabet recognition. Paper presented at the annual meeting of the American Educational Research Association, New Orleans, LA.

Under your care . . .
your students receive the best possible attention everyday!

Now that you use *Zaner-Bloser Handwriting*, we want to be sure you get the attention you need to make your job more successful. We have many communication channels available to meet your needs: phone our Customer Service Department at 1-800-421-3018, visit our website at www.zaner-bloser.com, use the card below to write to our editors, and use the card at the bottom to join our Customer Care Club.

Zaner-Bloser cares!

If you have any questions or comments concerning Zaner-Bloser instructional materials or questions about the teaching of handwriting, you may use this card to write to us. We will be happy to assist you in any way possible.

_____

_____

_____

_____

_____

Ms., Mr., etc. Name	Position	Grade Level(s)
School	School Address	
City	State	ZIP
( )	( )	( )
School Telephone	After Hours Phone	FAX

MH0327

Zaner-Bloser Customer Care Club

Join the Zaner-Bloser Customer Care Club and we'll make sure you stay up-to-date on current educational research and products. To enroll, you may return this card or call our Customer Care Club hotline at 1-800-387-2410. Upon enrollment, we'll get you started with a gift of information about teaching handwriting.

 **YES!** Please enroll me in the Zaner-Bloser Customer Care Club and send me the following pamphlet: **The Left-Handed Child in a Right-Handed World**

Zaner-Bloser

**2200 W. Fifth Ave.
PO Box 16764
Columbus, OH
43216-6764**

Ms., Mr., etc. Name	Position	Grade Level(s)
School	School Address	
City	State	ZIP
( )	( )	( )
School Telephone	After Hours Phone	FAX

**Visit our website:
www.zaner-bloser.com**

Please Note: **This program is for Zaner-Bloser customers only!**

MH0327

Zaner-Bloser

Customer Service: 1-800-421-3018

Customer Care Club: 1-800-387-2410

Website: www.zaner-bloser.com

BUSINESS REPLY MAIL

FIRST CLASS MAIL   PERMIT NO. 295   COLUMBUS, OH

POSTAGE WILL BE PAID BY ADDRESSEE

Zaner-Bloser

2200 W 5TH AVE
PO BOX 16764
COLUMBUS OH 43272-4176

BUSINESS REPLY MAIL

FIRST CLASS MAIL   PERMIT NO. 295   COLUMBUS, OH

POSTAGE WILL BE PAID BY ADDRESSEE

Zaner-Bloser

2200 W 5TH AVE
PO BOX 16764
COLUMBUS OH 43272-4176

Meeting Students' Individual Handwriting Needs

The Left-Handed Student

With proper instruction and encouragement, left-handed students can write as well as right-handed students. Three important techniques assist the left-handed student in writing.

Paper Position

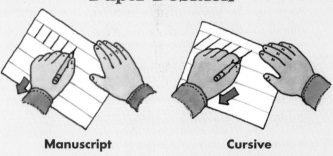

Manuscript   **Cursive**

For *manuscript writing,* the **lower right corner** of the paper should point toward the left of the body's mid-section.

For *cursive writing,* the **lower right corner** of the paper should point toward the body's midsection.

Downstrokes are pulled toward the left elbow.

Pencil Position

The top of the pencil should point toward the left elbow. The pen or pencil should be held at least one inch above the point. This allows students to see what they are writing.

Arm Position

Holding the left arm close to the body and keeping the hand below the line of writing prevents "hooking" the wrist and smearing the writing.

Students With Reversal Tendencies

- Downcurve
- Undercurve
- Slant
- Loop forward, undercurve

Directionality

A problem with directionality (moving from left to right across the page) interferes with a child's ability to form letters correctly and to write text that makes sense. To develop correct directionality, try these techniques:

- Provide opportunities for the child to write at the chalkboard within a confined area with frequent arrows as a reminder of left-to-right progression.
- Prepare sheets of paper on which the left edges and the beginning stroke of a letter, such as *b,* are colored green.

Letter Reversals

Determine which letters a student most often reverses. Make a list of these reversals and concentrate on them either on an individual basis or by grouping together the students who are reversing the same letters.

- Emphasize each step of the stroke description before the children write a letter.
- Provide a letter for tracing that has been colored according to stroke order. Repeat the stroke description with the children as they write the letter.
- Encourage the children to write the letter as they verbalize the stroke description.

Students With Other Special Needs

Success in handwriting is almost always a certainty if the initial instruction involves visual, auditory, and kinesthetic stimuli—a multisensory approach. Students need to develop a correct mental and motor image of the stroke, joining, letter, or word before they attempt to write. These techniques may help your students with special needs.

For the Kinesthetic Learner

- Walk out the letter strokes on the floor.
- Form letters in the air using full-arm movement.
- Make letter models with clay or string.
- Write strokes, letters, and joinings in sand.
- Use different writing instruments, such as crayons, markers, and varied sizes of pencils.
- Trace large strokes, letters, and joinings on the chalkboard and on paper—first with fingers, then with chalk or other media.
- Dip fingers in water and form letters and joinings on the chalkboard.

Remember that initial instruction, remediation, and maintenance for the student whose primary sensory modality is kinesthetic should be tactile, involving movement and the sense of touch.

For the Auditory Learner

- Verbalize each stroke in the letter as that letter is presented.
- Encourage the student to verbalize the letter strokes and to explain how strokes are alike and how they are different in the letterforms.
- Ask students to write random letters as you verbalize the strokes.
- Be consistent in the language you use to describe letters, strokes, shapes, and joinings.

Students whose primary sensory modality is auditory require instruction that enables them to listen and to verbalize.

For the Visual Learner

- Encourage students first to look at the letter as a whole and to ask themselves if the letter is tall or short, fat or skinny. Does all of the letter rest on the baseline, or is it a descender or a tall letter? How many and what kinds of strokes are in the letter?
- Have students look at each individual stroke carefully before they attempt to write the letter.

As a general rule, a student whose primary sensory modality is visual will have little difficulty in handwriting if instruction includes adequate visual stimuli.

For Learners With Attention Deficit Problems

Because they have difficulty focusing and maintaining attention, these students must concentrate on individual strokes in the letterforms. When they have learned the strokes, they can put them together to form letters, and then learn the joinings (in cursive) to write words.
- Give very short assignments.
- Supervise closely and give frequent encouragement.

Activities recommended for kinesthetic learners are appropriate for students with an attention deficit disorder.

General Coaching Tips for Teachers

- Teach a handwriting lesson daily, if possible, for no more than 15 minutes. Short, daily periods of instruction are preferable to longer, but less frequent, periods.
- Surround children with models of good handwriting. Set an example when you write on the chalkboard and on students' papers.
- Teach the letters through basic strokes.
- Emphasize one key to legibility at a time.
- Use appropriately ruled paper. Don't be afraid to increase the size of the grids for any student who is experiencing difficulty.
- Stress comfortable writing posture and pencil position. Increase the size of the pencil for students who "squeeze" the writing implement.
- Show the alternate method of holding the pencil, and allow students to choose the one that is better for them. (Refer to the alternate method shown on the Position Pages in the Teacher Edition.)
- Provide opportunities for children in the upper grades to use manuscript writing. Permit manuscript for some assignments, if children prefer manuscript to cursive.
- Encourage students with poor sustained motor control to use conventional manuscript, with frequent lifts, if continuous manuscript is difficult for them.

Zaner-Bloser
Handwriting
With continuous-stroke alphabet

Author

Clinton S. Hackney

Contributing Authors

Pamela J. Farris
Janice T. Jones
Linda Leonard Lamme

Zaner Bloser, Inc.

P.O. Box 16764
Columbus, Ohio 43216-6764

Author

Clinton S. Hackney, Ed.D.

Contributing Authors

Pamela J. Farris, Ph.D.
Janice T. Jones, M.A.
Linda Leonard Lamme, Ph.D.

Reviewers

Judy L. Bausch, Columbus, Georgia
Cherlynn Bruce, Conroe, Texas
Karen H. Burke, Director of Curriculum and Instruction, Bar Mills, Maine
Anne Chamberlin, Lynchburg, Virginia
Carol J. Fuhler, Flagstaff, Arizona
Deborah D. Gallagher, Gainesville, Florida
Kathleen Harrington, Redford, Michigan
Rebecca James, East Greenbush, New York
Gerald R. Maeckelbergh, Principal, Blaine, Minnesota
Bessie B. Peabody, Principal, East St. Louis, Illinois

Marilyn S. Petruska, Coraopolis, Pennsylvania
Sharon Ralph, Nashville, Tennessee
Linda E. Ritchie, Birmingham, Alabama
Roberta Hogan Royer, North Canton, Ohio
Marion Redmond Starks, Baltimore, Maryland
Elizabeth J. Taglieri, Lake Zurich, Illinois
Claudia Williams, Lewisburg, West Virginia

Credits

Art: Diane Blasius: 4, 30, 31, 38, 40–41, 46–47, 52, 58–59, 64, 80–81, 84–85, 88; Gloria Elliott: 3–4, 20–23, 98–101; Kristen Goeters: 44–45, 48–49, 52, 60–61, 64, 66–69, 76–77, 86–87, 88; Michael Grejniec: 102–103, 113–120; Tom Leonard: 6–7, 26–27, 32–33, 38, 42–43, 50–52, 56–57, 64, 70–71, 78–79, 88; Daniel Moreton: 3, 5, 25, 27, 29, 31, 35, 41, 43, 45, 47, 49, 51, 57, 61, 63, 67, 69, 71, 73, 77, 79, 81, 83, 85, 87, 95; Diane Paterson: 112; Gail Piazza: 3, 24–25, 28–29, 34–35, 38, 62–64, 72–73, 82–83, 88; Andy San Diego: 3, 36–37, 39, 53–54, 65, 75, 89, 90

Photos: John Lei/OPC: 8–9, 21, 23; Stephen Ogilvy: 3–7, 10–18, 20, 22, 24–94, 96–109

Developed by Kirchoff/Wohlberg, Inc., in cooperation with Zaner-Bloser Publishers

Cover illustration by Daniel Moreton

ISBN 0-88085-945-8

CONTENTS

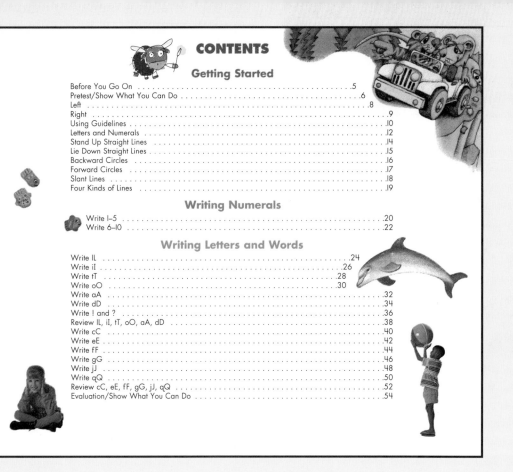

Getting Started

Before You Go On 5
Pretest/Show What You Can Do 6
Left 8
Right 9
Using Guidelines 10
Letters and Numerals 12
Stand Up Straight Lines 14
Lie Down Straight Lines 15
Backward Circles 16
Forward Circles 17
Slant Lines 18
Four Kinds of Lines 19

Writing Numerals

Write 1–5 20
Write 6–10 22

Writing Letters and Words

Write lL 24
Write iI 26
Write tT 28
Write oO 30
Write aA 32
Write dD 34
Write ! and ? 36
Review lL, iI, tT, oO, aA, dD 38
Write cC 40
Write eE 42
Write fF 44
Write gG 46
Write jJ 48
Write qQ 50
Review cC, eE, fF, gG, jJ, qQ 52
Evaluation/Show What You Can Do 54

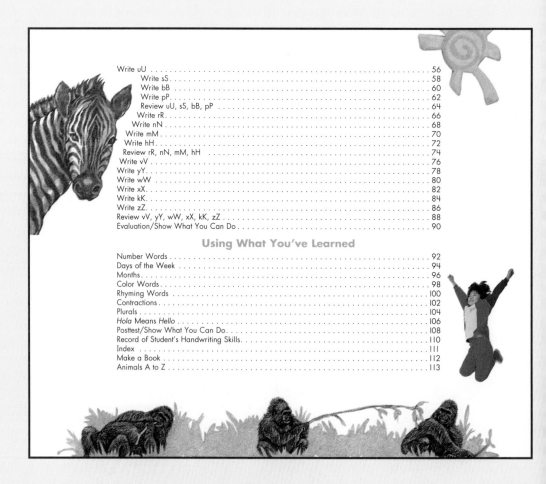

Write uU 56
Write sS 58
Write bB 60
Write pP 62
Review uU, sS, bB, pP 64
Write rR 66
Write nN 68
Write mM 70
Write hH 72
Review rR, nN, mM, hH 74
Write vV 76
Write yY 78
Write wW 80
Write xX 82
Write kK 84
Write zZ 86
Review vV, yY, wW, xX, kK, zZ 88
Evaluation/Show What You Can Do 90

Using What You've Learned

Number Words 92
Days of the Week 94
Months 96
Color Words 98
Rhyming Words 100
Contractions 102
Plurals 104
Hola Means *Hello* 106
Posttest/Show What You Can Do 108
Record of Student's Handwriting Skills 110
Index 111
Make a Book 112
Animals A to Z 113

Before You Go On . . .

Hi!

We're here to help you write!

5

Practice Masters

- Getting Started, 1–16
- Numerals, 17–18
- Letters, 19–70
- Record of Student's Handwriting Skills, 71
- Certificates, 72–74
- Letter to Parents—English, 75, 77, 79
- Letter to Parents—Spanish, 76, 78, 80
- Alphabet—English, 81
- Alphabet—Spanish, 82
- Stroke Descriptions—English, 83–86
- Stroke Descriptions—Spanish, 87–90
- Write in Spanish, 91–109
- Zaner-Bloser Handwriting Grid, 110

HOW THIS BOOK IS ORGANIZED

The **Getting Started** pages are important for laying a foundation for writing. Children will also be learning the vocabulary in this handwriting program.

In **Writing Numerals**, children are introduced to numerals 1 through 10.

Lowercase and uppercase letters are introduced together in **Writing Letters and Words**. The letter sequence is determined by common elements of the lowercase letters.

Finally, children apply their knowledge in **Using What You've Learned**, which includes words in categories and words in several languages.

Note that models are provided for all writing, and children have space to write directly beneath the models. **On Your Own** encourages children to write about their own experiences.

It is suggested that children keep a writing notebook or folder of the writing they do for themselves and for others.

Use this introductory page with your class as an invitation to the Zaner-Bloser handwriting program. Call attention to the speech balloons that show what each child is saying. Tell children that they will be seeing these children and other helpers throughout the book.

Explain to children that in this book they will learn how to write letters, words, and sentences. They will also discover ways to help make their writing easy to read.

PRACTICE MASTER 1

Draw a picture of yourself.

Write your name.

Copyright © Zaner-Bloser, Inc.   PRACTICE MASTER 1

BEGIN WITH A SONG

Write "The Alphabet Song" on chart paper. As you point to the letters, invite children to sing this familiar song with you.

A-B-C-D-E-F-G
H-I-J-K
L-M-N-O-P
Q-R-S
T-U-V
W-X-Y and Z
Now I know my
    ABC's
Next time won't you
    sing with me?

BOOKS FOR SHARING

Harold and the Purple Crayon
by Crockett Johnson

Chicka Chicka Boom Boom
by Bill Martin Jr and John Archambault

Eating the Alphabet Fruits and Vegetables from A to Z
by Lois Ehlert

Applebet: An ABC
by Clyde Watson

Have You Ever Seen . . . ?
An ABC Book
by Beau Gardner

Fish Eyes
A Book You Can Count On
by Lois Ehlert

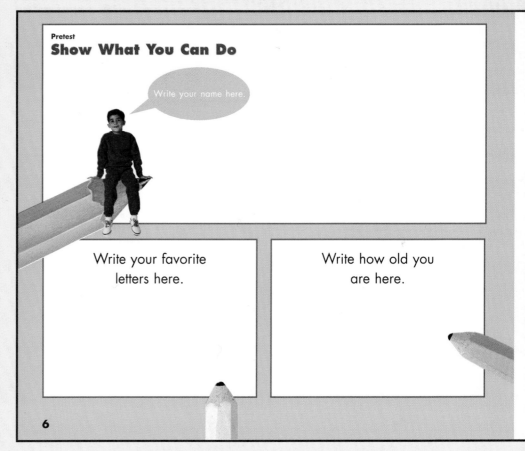

Pretest
Show What You Can Do

Write your name here.

Write your favorite letters here.

Write how old you are here.

6

Tell children that during handwriting time they will be learning to write the letters of the alphabet and the numerals.

Preview the book with the children. Explain that the first thing they will do is show what they can write.

Work through these pages with the children.

Help children locate the writing spaces for their name, favorite letters, and age. Discuss ideas for writing for page 7.

EVALUATE

Observe how children write their names and ages. Note that many children may still be writing their names in all uppercase letters.

Children may have been taught to write some, or all, of the alphabet letters and numerals in kindergarten. You may use these pages as a pretest to help you assess each child's present handwriting skills.

Show what else you can write here.

MY NAME

Invite children to write their names with crayon on drawing paper. Suggest they use different colors for the letters. Have them paint over the paper with thin tempera paint. The crayoned letters will resist the paint, and the name will show through. (visual)

COACHING HINT

Make a desktop nametag for each child in your class using tagboard or self-adhesive ruled name strips. Tape the nametags to the children's desks so they can use them as writing models. (visual)

Children whose writing is large should be given many opportunities to write at the chalkboard, on the classified ad section of the newspaper, or on wide-ruled newsprint. A writing crayon is good for large writing. (kinesthetic)

PRACTICE MASTER 2

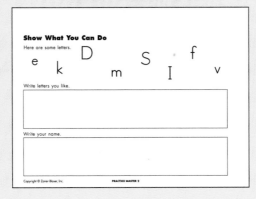

Show What You Can Do

Here are some letters.

e   k   D   m   S   I   f   v

Write letters you like.

Write your name.

Copyright © Zaner-Bloser, Inc.   PRACTICE MASTER 2

PRACTICE MASTER 3

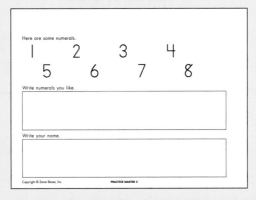

Here are some numerals.

1   2   3   4
5   6   7   8

Write numerals you like.

Write your name.

Copyright © Zaner-Bloser, Inc.   PRACTICE MASTER 3

ALIKE AND DIFFERENT

Prepare two sets of cards, each with numerals from 1 to 10, for a matching game. Show children how to play the game by turning all the cards facedown. Have the first player choose two cards. If the numerals match, have that child name the numeral, trace it, and keep the pair in his or her pile. Players take turns, and the player with the most pairs wins. (visual)

BEGIN WITH A SONG

Sing "The Alphabet Song " together to signal the beginning of handwriting time.

Then invite children to stand in a circle and sing and play "Looby-Loo."

Here we dance Looby-loo,
Here we dance Looby-light.
Here we dance Looby-loo,
All on a Saturday night.

I put my *right hand* in,
I put my *right hand* out.
I give my *right hand* a
    shake, shake, shake,
And turn myself about.

Repeat using the words *left hand, right foot, left foot, head,* and *whole self.*

Left

8

If you write with your left hand . . .
Sit up tall.
Hold your pencil like this.
Slant your paper.

PENCIL POSITION

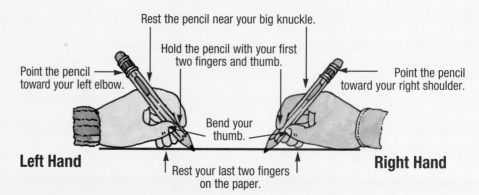

Rest the pencil near your big knuckle.

Hold the pencil with your first two fingers and thumb.

Point the pencil toward your left elbow.

Point the pencil toward your right shoulder.

Bend your thumb.

Rest your last two fingers on the paper.

Left Hand

Right Hand

Work through these pages with the children.

Show children how the index finger and thumb of the left hand make an **L** for *left.* Have them find the **L** on their left hands.

Demonstrate how to place both arms on the desk, with only the elbows off the desk, and to sit up straight.

Give out pencils and help children determine whether they usually write or draw with their left hand or their right hand.

Demonstrate the correct way to hold a pencil for both left- and right-handers.

Distribute paper with writing lines and help children follow the directions for proper paper position.

PAPER POSITION

Let children use what they have learned by writing their names or some letters on the paper.

See the Handwriting Positions Wall Chart for more information.

If you write with your right hand . . .

Sit up tall.

Hold your pencil like this.

Keep your paper straight.

Right

LEFT HAND, RIGHT HAND

Have children help each other trace the shape of their own left and right hands on construction paper. Then direct children to cut them out and paste them on another sheet of paper. Demonstrate how to write L on the left hand and R on the right hand. Ask children to draw a ring on one finger of the hand they use for writing. (kinesthetic, visual)

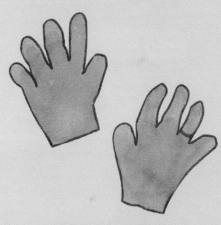

SIMON SAYS

To play this variation of "Simon Says," give children directions that include the words *left* and *right*. Have them stand facing you. Remind them to follow the direction only when they hear "Simon says." Here are some ideas:

Simon says, "Touch your nose with your right hand."

"Touch your chin with your left hand."

Simon says, "Take two steps to the left."

(auditory, kinesthetic)

COACHING HINT

Right-handed teachers will better understand left-handed children if they practice the left-handed position themselves. The Zaner-Bloser Writing Frame can be used to show good hand position because the hand automatically settles into the correct position. Group left-handers together for instruction if you can do so without calling attention to the practice. They should be seated to the left of the chalkboard.

Children who have difficulty with the traditional pencil position may prefer the alternate method of holding the pencil between the first and second fingers.

PRACTICE MASTER 4

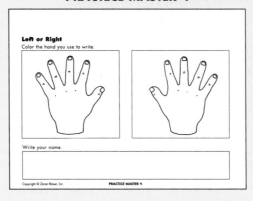

Left or Right
Color the hand you use to write.

Write your name.

Copyright © Zaner-Bloser, Inc.   PRACTICE MASTER 4

PRACTICE MASTER 5

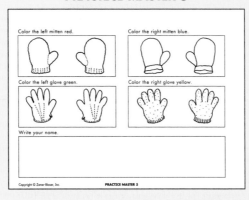

Color the left mitten red.   Color the right mitten blue.

Color the left glove green.   Color the right glove yellow.

Write your name.

Copyright © Zaner-Bloser, Inc.   PRACTICE MASTER 5

Write **A**, **B**, and **C** on guidelines on the chalk-board.

Sing "The Alphabet Song," replacing the last lines with these:

I shall write my ABC's,
On the guidelines that I see.

Explain that using guidelines will help them write better letters. Help them locate and name the headline, midline, and baseline.

Using Guidelines
Where are the letters?

Headline

Midline

Baseline

 10

Work through these pages with the children.

Guide children in locating and naming each guideline. Have them name its color and tell whether the line is solid or broken.

Have children locate the photo of the child standing between the headline and base-line. Introduce the tall letters. Have children trace **T** and **h.** Explain that **T** and **h** are tall letters. They touch both the headline and the baseline. Ask children for other examples of tall letters. Call attention to the fact that all uppercase letters are tall.

Next, have children locate the photo of the child sitting between the midline and base-line. Introduce the short letters. Have children trace **e**. Explain that **e** is a short letter. It does not go above the midline and touches the baseline. Ask children for examples of other short letters.

Then, have children locate the photo of the child sitting between the midline and base-line with legs that go below the baseline. Point out that some short letters, like **g**, go below the baseline and touch the headline of the next writing line. Ask children for examples of short letters that go below the baseline.

Note: Photographs of children will appear on the guidelines of each of the letter pages. Their purpose is to act as locators, help children use the guidelines correctly, and help with horizontal alignment.

Headline

Midline

Baseline

FUN WITH GUIDELINES

Draw guidelines with chalk on the playground hardtop or make them with masking tape on the floor. Have children sit in front of the guidelines. Ask them to follow directions similar to these:

Hop along the headline.

Lie on the midline.

Sit on the baseline.

Sit in the space below the baseline.

Walk the baseline on tiptoes.

Invite children to say directions for classmates to follow. (auditory, kinesthetic)

EVALUATE

Write two tall letters on the chalkboard, one of which touches the guidelines correctly and the other with errors. Ask children to evaluate the two letters by circling the correct one. Do the same with two short letters and with short letters that go below the baseline.

COACHING HINT

Distribute sheets of the lined writing paper children will be using in order to familiarize them with the guidelines. Help them locate the first set of guidelines. Demonstrate and have children follow along as you trace the headline with a blue crayon, the broken midline with blue, and the baseline with red. (visual, kinesthetic)

PRACTICE MASTER 6

Using Guidelines

Headline / Midline / Baseline

a b c d e f g h

Which letter is tall? Circle it. c C e a

Which letter is short? Circle it. M N o P

Which letter goes below the baseline? Circle it. h i j k

Write your name.

Copyright © Zaner-Bloser, Inc.   PRACTICE MASTER 6

PRACTICE MASTER 7

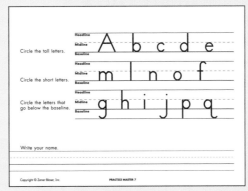

Circle the tall letters. A b c d e

Circle the short letters. m l n o f

Circle the letters that go below the baseline. g h i j p q

Write your name.

Copyright © Zaner-Bloser, Inc.   PRACTICE MASTER 7

GUESS THE LETTER

Make sure an alphabet is on display for children to refer to when you play this riddle game about lowercase alphabet letters. Begin by saying, *I am thinking of a letter. It is tall. It comes after s. What is it?* Repeat for different letters. Then have children make up their own riddles. (auditory, visual)

Before you sing, have children open their books to the alphabet and numeral chart on pages 12 and 13. Ask them to look at the letters and join in singing "The Alphabet Song."

Now try this letter identification game. Sing the following words to the tune of "Where Is Thumbkin?" Ask children to point to the letters named.

Where is uppercase **B**?
Where is lowercase **b**?
Here they are!
Here they are!

Now find uppercase **T**.
Now find lowercase **t**.
Hip-hip-hooray!
Hip-hip-hooray!

Invite children to look at the numerals on the page and to point to each numeral as you recite the following rhyme.

One potato, two potato,
Three potato, four,
Five potato, six potato,
Seven potato, more.
Eight potato, nine potato,
Ten potato, too.
Counting all the numbers,
Is what I like to do.

Letters **and** Numerals

Aa Bb Cc Dd Ee
Ff Gg Hh Ii Jj Kk
Ll Mm Nn Oo

Trace the uppercase letter that begins your name.
Trace the lowercase letters in your name.

 12

EVALUATE

Invite children to compare the letters they wrote with the models they traced in the alphabet.

To help children evaluate their writing, ask questions such as these:

Did you begin your name with an uppercase letter?
Does your uppercase letter touch the headline?
Does your uppercase letter touch the baseline?

Invite children to talk about the letters they used and how the guidelines helped them.

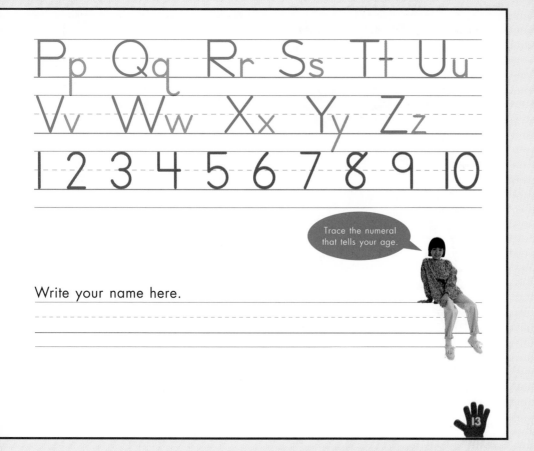

Pp Qq Rr Ss Tt Uu Vv Ww Xx Yy Zz

1 2 3 4 5 6 7 8 9 10

Trace the numeral that tells your age.

Write your name here.

TACTILE LETTERS

Involve children in making a set of tactile alphabet letter cards for the writing center. Print each letter pair (uppercase and lowercase) on a blank index card and distribute the cards. Invite children to glue seeds, glitter, colored sand, or beans to the outline of each letter. When the letters are complete, have children take turns touching and naming a letter pair. (kinesthetic)

ALPHABET SWITCH

Have children sit on chairs in a circle. Give each child a different lowercase letter card. Choose one child to stand in the center without a card. Call out the names of two letters and then say "Alphabet Switch." The children with the letters named will change places, while the child in the middle tries to get a seat. After each exchange, have children name the letters. (auditory, visual)

COACHING HINT

Refer children to these pages often as a guide for writing. Children will find them especially helpful when they write independently.

The development of self-evaluation skills is an important goal of handwriting instruction. It helps children become independent learners. By having children compare their letters with models, you have already begun this process. Be patient. Some children will be more able than others to evaluate their writing.

Practice Masters 81–82 show the alphabet in English and Spanish.

PRACTICE MASTER 8

Uppercase Letters

Circle the uppercase letter that begins your name.

A B C D E F G H I J
K L M N O P Q R S T
U V W X Y Z

Trace and circle the uppercase letter that begins each name.

Carl   Lauren   Zach

Write your name.

PRACTICE MASTER 9

Lowercase Letters and Numerals

Circle the lowercase letters in your name.

a b c d e f g h i j
k l m n o p q r s t
u v w x y z

Trace and circle the numeral that tells your age.

1 2 3 4 5 6 7 8 9 10

Write your name.

Sing "The Alphabet Song," replacing the last two lines with the following.

When you see the ABC's,
Look for some straight lines
with me.

Ask children to tell what kind of lines are mentioned.

Tell children they will be looking for two kinds of straight lines. One line stands up straight. Ask children to stand up straight. Point out that a stand up straight line might be drawn from the top of their heads to the bottom of their feet.

Explain that the other straight line is a lie down straight line. Ask children to stand with arms outstretched. Point out that a lie down straight line might be drawn from their left hand to their right.

MODEL

Model stand up straight and lie down straight lines in the air and have children copy you.

14

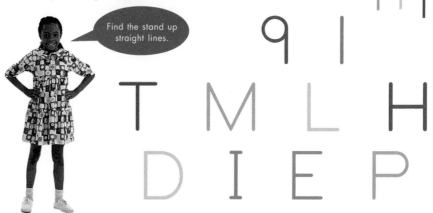

Stand Up Straight Lines

Here are some letters and numerals with stand up straight lines.

Find the stand up straight lines.

9 1 l l l l

T M L H

D I E P

Write your name.

- -

Are there any lines like this l in your name?   Yes   No

14

Work through these pages with the children.

Stand Up Straight Lines

Help children find the stand up straight lines in the letters and numerals. Have them trace each stand up straight line from top to bottom with a finger, crayon, or pencil.

Invite children to write some stand up straight lines on the page.

Ask children to count the stand up straight lines in their names.

Lie Down Straight Lines

Here are some letters and numerals with lie down straight lines.

I Z 4 5 E
L H T A F

Find the lie down straight lines.

Write your name.

Are there any lines like this — in your name?   Yes   No

Lie Down Straight Lines

Help children find the lie down straight lines. Then have them trace each lie down straight line from left to right.

Invite children to write some lie down straight lines of their own.

Ask children to count the lie down straight lines in their names.

COACHING HINT

Have children look around the room for objects formed with lines. Help them determine whether a line is horizontal or vertical and describe it using the terms *stand up straight* or *lie down straight*. If possible, have them trace the lines as well. (visual)

PRACTICE MASTER 10

Look for stand up straight lines.   I | |

Trace the stand up straight lines in each letter or numeral.

I   t   h   i   b   4   5
D   K   F   N   P   9

Write stand up straight lines.

Write your name.

Copyright © Zaner-Bloser, Inc.   PRACTICE MASTER 10

PRACTICE MASTER 11

Look for lie down straight lines.   — _ —

Trace the lie down straight lines in each letter or numeral.

e   f   t   z   2   5
A   7   F   H   E   4   G

Write lie down straight lines.

Write your name.

Copyright © Zaner-Bloser, Inc.   PRACTICE MASTER 11

LINES, LINES, LINES

Help children fold drawing paper into two sections. Ask them to draw stand up straight lines in a variety of colors in one section and lie down straight lines in the other. Provide crayons, markers, colored chalk, or paint. Have children discuss their lines with a partner and circle their longest and shortest lines. Encourage them to count the number of lines of a certain color and the total number of lines. (visual)

CRAFT STICK LETTERS

Distribute craft sticks, glue, and construction paper for children to use to make letters. Ask children which letters have only stand up straight and lie down straight lines (E, F, H, I, L, l, T, t) and write these letters on the chalkboard. Demonstrate how to place the sticks on construction paper to form a letter and to glue it in place. Have children share their completed letters. (visual, kinesthetic)

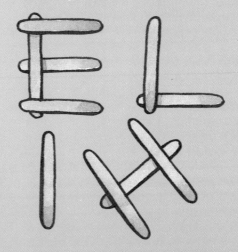

Sing "The Alphabet Song," replacing the last two lines with the following.

When you see the ABC's,
Look for circle lines
with me.

Ask children to tell what kind of lines are mentioned.

Draw two circles on the chalkboard. Show where a backward circle line begins by marking a starting place, at about one o'clock, with a star. Ask children to begin at the star and use their index fingers to trace over the line.

Show where a forward circle line begins by marking a starting place, at about nine o'clock, with a star. Ask children to begin at the star and use their index fingers to trace over the line.

MODEL
Use your arm to model making backward circles (left) and forward circles (right) and have children copy you.

16

Backward Circles
Here are some letters and numerals with backward circle lines.

Find the backward circle lines.

C O Q
G 9 8

Write your name.

_____

_ _

_____

Does your name have letters with C or O ? Yes   No

 16

Work through these pages with the children.

Backward Circles

Help children find the backward circle lines in the letters and numerals on this page. Have them trace each circle line with a finger, crayon, or pencil. Some children will need help with direction.

Invite children to make some backward circle lines on the page.

Ask children to name the letters in their names that have backward circle lines.

Forward Circles

Here are some letters and numerals with forward circle lines.

Find the forward circle lines.

D P R 3

2 B 5

Write your name.

Does your name have letters with) ? Yes   No

17

Forward Circles

Help children find the forward circle lines. Have them trace each circle line. Give help with direction.

Invite children to make some forward circle lines.

Ask children to name the letters in their names that have forward circle lines.

COACHING HINT

Use an overhead projector to project stand up straight, lie down straight, and backward and forward circle lines on the chalkboard. Ask children to wet their fingers in a cup of water and trace the enlarged lines on the chalkboard. (kinesthetic)

PRACTICE MASTER 12

Look for backward circle lines. C O
Trace the backward circle lines in each letter or numeral.

o   a   d   O   Q

g   q   6   9   G

Write backward circle lines.

Write your name.

Copyright © Zaner-Bloser, Inc.   PRACTICE MASTER 12

PRACTICE MASTER 13

Look for forward circle lines. ⊃ ○
Trace the forward circle lines in each letter or numeral.

b   p   P   5   3

R   D   2   B

Write forward circle lines.

Write your name.

Copyright © Zaner-Bloser, Inc.   PRACTICE MASTER 13

CIRCLES ARE ROUND

Draw a large circle on a sheet of paper. Put a star for the start and an arrow pointing a direction for cutting. Duplicate a circle for each child. Have children help each other cut out the circles. Talk about things that are round and ask children to draw round things on their circles. (kinesthetic)

CIRCLE LEFT, CIRCLE RIGHT

Invite children to join hands and form a circle. Review that a circle can go backward, to the left, or forward, to the right. Play some music and have children move in a circle. Stop the music and have them change direction. Then chant this rhyme as you lead children in following the words and circling around.

Circle left, circle left.
    Circle all around.
Circle right, circle right.
    Stop and look around.
(auditory, kinesthetic)

17

Sing "The Alphabet Song," replacing the last two lines with the following.

When you see the ABC's,
Look for some slant
lines with me.

Ask children to tell what kind of lines are mentioned. Give each child a craft stick. Ask children to make the stick stand up straight and then to lie down straight. Demonstrate how to make the stick slant right, then left. Ask children to copy you. Explain that they will be looking for lines that slant right or left.

MODEL

Model in the air a line that slants right and then a line that slants left and have children copy you. Next, have them imitate as you make an **X** to show a letter that has both a slant right and a slant left line.

18

Slant Lines

Here are some letters and a numeral with slant lines.

Find the slant lines.

A K M 7

W X Y V

Write your name.

Is there a \ or / in your name? Yes   No

18

Work through these pages with the children.

Slant Lines

Help children find the slant lines in the letters and numeral. Have them trace each slant line with a finger, crayon, or pencil.

Invite children to make some slant lines on the page.

Ask children to name the letters with slant lines in their names. Help them determine whether a line slants right or left.

Four Kinds of Lines

Discuss with children why knowing about these four lines will help them as they begin to write letters.

EVALUATE

Guide children in evaluating their lines by asking questions such as these:

Are your stand up straight lines straight?
Are your lie down straight lines straight?
Are your backward circle and forward circle lines round?
Are your slant lines straight?

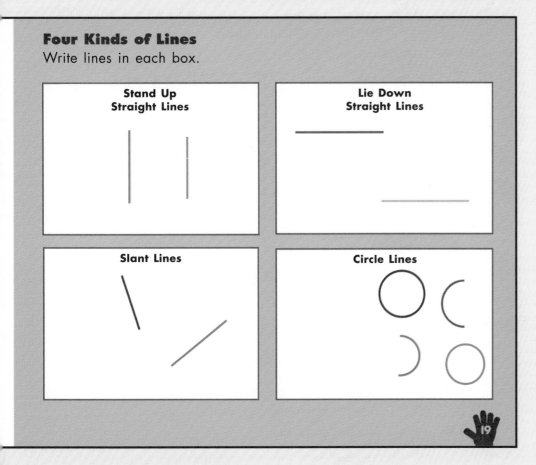

Four Kinds of Lines
Write lines in each box.

Stand Up Straight Lines

Lie Down Straight Lines

Slant Lines

Circle Lines

BEFORE YOU GO ON...

The purpose of this handwriting program is to help children write legibly. As handwriting instruction progresses, you will find many opportunities for children to evaluate their writing by using the keys to legibility.

Keys to Legibility
size and shape
slant
spacing

Help children become confident in their judgments. Remember that the goal of self-evaluation is improvement.

PRACTICE MASTER 15

Look for slant right lines. \\ \\ \\

Trace the slant right lines in each letter.

A N M Q R X
K v w Y W

Write slant right lines.

Write your name.

PRACTICE MASTER 14

Look for slant left lines. // // //

Trace the slant left lines in each letter or numeral.

A z Y 7 Z X
2 x y K k

Write slant left lines.

Write your name.

PRACTICE MASTER 16

Write these lines.

Draw a picture using 4 kinds of lines.

Write your name.

FUN and GameS

CRAZY CRITTERS
Have children use circle and slant strokes to draw pictures of insects or animals. Caterpillars and bees are possible suggestions to get them started. (visual)

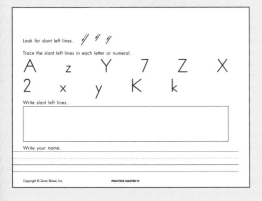

CHALKBOARD DRAWING
Have children take turns at the chalkboard as you give these directions for drawing a house.

Make the outside walls with stand up straight lines.

Make the floor with a lie down straight line.

Make the windows with lie down straight lines and circle forward or backward lines.

Make the roof with slant lines, left and right.

Make the bushes with backward or forward circles.

(auditory, kinesthetic)

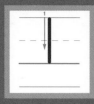

Touch the headline; pull down straight to the baseline.

Touch below the headline; curve forward (right); slant left to the baseline. Slide right.

Touch below the headline; curve forward (right) to the midline; curve forward (right), ending above the baseline.

Touch the headline; pull down straight to the midline. Slide right. Lift. Move to the right and touch the headline; pull down straight to the baseline.

Touch the headline; pull down straight to the midline. Circle forward (right), ending above the baseline. Lift. Touch the headline; slide right.

20

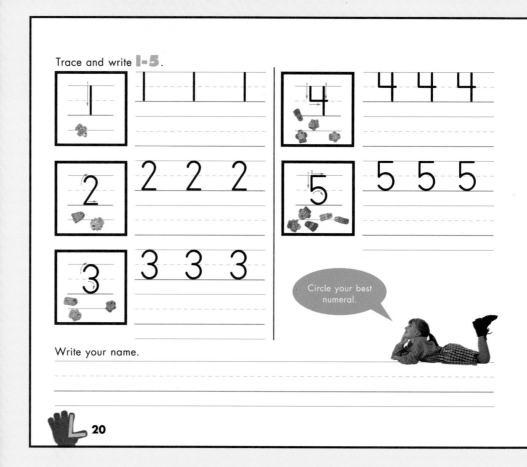

Trace and write 1-5.

Circle your best numeral.

Write your name.

20

MODEL

Write the numeral 1 on guidelines as you say the stroke descriptions. Model writing 1 in the air as you repeat the descriptions. Have children echo them as they write 1 in the air with you. Follow the same procedure for 2, 3, 4, and 5.

PRACTICE

Let children practice writing 1, 2, 3, 4, and 5 on laminated writing cards or slates before they write on the pages.

EVALUATE

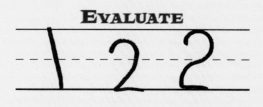

To help children evaluate their writing of numerals, ask questions such as these:
Is the pull down straight stroke in your 1 straight?

Does your 2 begin below the headline?
Is the slant left stroke in your 2 straight?

Does the slide right stroke in your 2 rest on the baseline?

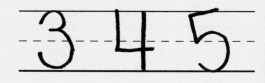

Is your 3 about the same width as the model?
Are both parts of your 3 the same size?
Does your 3 touch the headline and baseline?

Are the strokes in your 4 straight?
Do both pull down straight strokes in your 4 touch the headline?
Is your slide right stroke on the midline?

Is your 5 straight up and down?

Write the numerals to finish the rhyme.

1 2 3 4 5

I caught a fish alive.

On Your Own Write a numeral. Draw a picture to show how many.

Circle your best numeral.

WRITE NUMERALS

Read aloud the rhyme on the student page, inviting children to hold up fingers as each numeral is named. Have them point to each numeral, noting how it touches both the headline and baseline. Ask questions to focus attention on the strokes and placement on guidelines. After children write, have them compare their numerals with the models. Invite them to show the numeral they wrote and its accompanying picture .

COACHING HINT

Children vary in their ability to write within the confines of a designated area. Some children may not be ready to use lined paper. The teacher should decide what type of paper is best for individuals.

PRACTICE MASTER 17

Trace and write 1–5.   Write how many.

1   O
2   OO
3   OOO
4   OOOO
5   OOOOO

Write your name.

NUMBER CHART

Cut colored paper into one-inch squares. Have children write the numerals **1** through **5** down the left side of paper. Invite them to paste squares in rows going across—one square next to **1**, two squares next to **2**, and so on. Review the completed charts together. (visual, kinesthetic)

TRACE AND COUNT

Provide play dough or clay and fill several bags with paper shapes, buttons, or other small items. Invite pairs of children to play a game: One child forms a numeral from 1 to 5 from the dough or clay, saying the strokes. The other child traces the numeral and counts out that number of objects from the bag. Then children change roles. (kinesthetic, visual)

21

Touch the headline; curve down to the baseline; curve up to the midline and around to close the circle.

Touch the headline; slide right. Slant left to the baseline.

Touch below the headline; curve back (left); curve forward (right), touching the baseline; slant up (right) to the headline.

Touch below the headline; circle back (left) all the way around. Pull down straight to the baseline.

Touch the headline; pull down straight to the baseline. Lift. Touch the headline; curve down to the baseline; curve up to the headline.

Trace and write **6-10**.

Circle your best numeral.

Write your name.

22

MODEL

Write the numeral **6** on guidelines as you say the stroke descriptions. Have children use their index fingers to write **6** on their desks as you repeat the descriptions. Follow the same procedure for **7**, **8**, **9**, and **10**.

PRACTICE

Let children practice writing **6**, **7**, **8**, **9**, and **10** on laminated writing cards or slates before they write on the pages.

EVALUATE

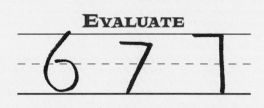

To help children evaluate their writing of numerals, ask questions such as these:
Does your **6** begin at the headline with a curve down stroke?
Does your **6** have a closed circle?

Does your **7** begin on the headline and end on the baseline?
Are both strokes of your **7** straight?

Does your **8** begin below the headline?
Does the slant stroke in your **8** connect with the beginning stroke?
Are the curves of your **8** about the same size?

Does your **9** have a round backward circle?
Is your **9** straight up and down?

Is there a space between **1** and **0** in your **10**?
Does your **10** touch the headline and baseline?

Write the numerals to finish the rhyme.

6 7 8 9 10

I let it go again.

On Your Own
Write a numeral. Draw a picture to show how many.

Circle your best numeral.

23

USE NUMERALS

Brainstorm with children and list places where they see numerals, such as on houses, calendars, highways, street signs, and book pages. Then discuss ways we use numbers. Duplicate questions that can be answered with numerals. Have children write the numeral that answers each question on paper with guidelines. Questions might include these:

How old are you?
How many brothers do you have?
What number is on your house or apartment?
What day is your birthday?
(visual)

WRITE NUMERALS

Recall the first part of the rhyme with the children. Read the second part of the rhyme aloud, inviting children to hold up fingers as each numeral is named. Say the stroke descriptions used to form one of the numerals and ask them to name that numeral. After children write, have them compare their numerals with the models. Then have them share their numerals and pictures.

PRACTICE MASTER 18

Trace and write 6–10.	Write how many.
6	○○○ ○○○
7	○○○ ○○○○
8	○○○○ ○○○○
9	○○○○ ○○○○○
10	○○○○○ ○○○○○

Write your name.

Copyright © Zaner-Bloser, Inc.   PRACTICE MASTER 18

COACHING HINT

Concentrate on the use of the guidelines for correct numeral formation. As you demonstrate on the chalkboard, have the children do the following on paper with guidelines.

• Draw over the baseline with red crayon.
• Draw over the headline with blue crayon.
• Draw over the midline with green crayon. (visual, kinesthetic)

COUNT AND WRITE

Prepare squares of paper with or without guidelines. Pair children and tell one child to arrange small objects such as blocks, buttons, or seeds into a group. Ask the other child to write the numeral that shows how many. Have children exchange tasks. (visual, kinesthetic)

23

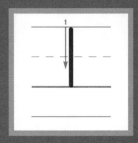

Touch the headline; pull down straight to the baseline.

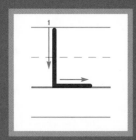

Touch the headline; pull down straight to the baseline. Slide right.

MODEL

Write **I** on guidelines as you say the stroke descriptions. Model writing **I** in the air as you repeat the descriptions. Have children echo them as they write **I** in the air with you. Follow the same procedure for **L**.

PRACTICE

Let children practice writing **I** and **L** on laminated writing cards or slates before they write on the pages.

24

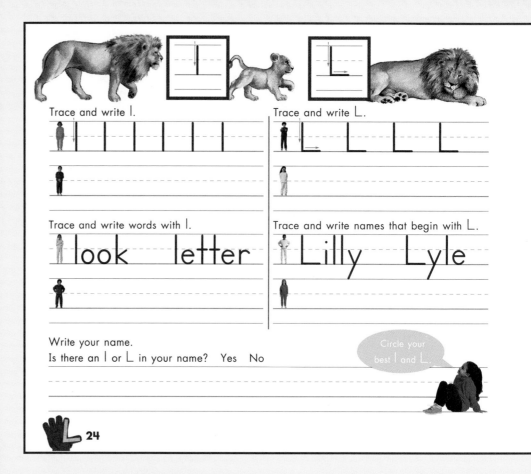

Trace and write I.

Trace and write L.

Trace and write words with I.

look letter

Trace and write names that begin with L.

Lilly Lyle

Write your name.
Is there an I or L in your name?   Yes   No

Circle your best I and L.

24

EVALUATE

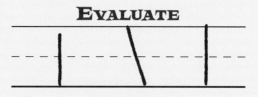

To help children evaluate their writing, ask questions such as these:
Does your **I** begin at the headline?
Does your **I** rest on the baseline?
Is your **I** straight up and down?

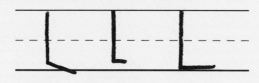

Are your strokes straight?
Does your **L** stop at the baseline before the slide right?
Is your slide right on the baseline?

Note: In each Evaluate section, the first two letterforms in each group illustrate common problems in letter formation. The third letter is an acceptable letterform written by a child.

BETTER LETTERS

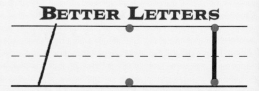

To help children write a vertical **I**, check that the paper is positioned correctly. Have them practice pulling their index fingers straight down from the headline to the baseline. Then place a dot for *start* and a dot for *stop*. Say the stroke descriptions as the children write **I**.

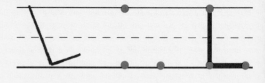

To help children write an **L** that rests on the baseline, demonstrate where to stop before making the slide right stroke. Remind them not to lift the pencil.

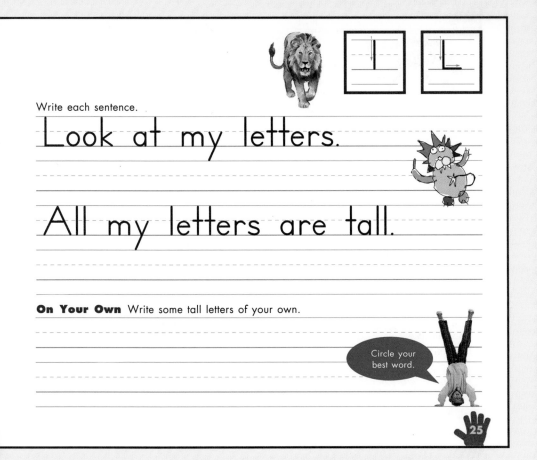

Write each sentence.

Look at my letters.

All my letters are tall.

On Your Own Write some tall letters of your own.

Circle your best word.

25

PHONICS CONNECTION

Have children make a lollipop by attaching a colored circle to a craft stick. After everyone agrees that *lollipop* begins with l, ask children to write an l on one side of the colored circle. Remind them that l begins the word *lion*. Then say other words, such as *let, like, pet, little,* and *book*. Tell them to hold up their lollipops with the l side facing you if the word you say begins like *lion*. Tell them to show the blank side if the word does not begin like *lion*. Repeat with **L** lollipops and names of people. (auditory, visual)

WRITE SENTENCES

Before children write the two sentences on the page, call attention to the space between letters in each word. Point out that there is more space between words than between letters in a word. After they write, have them evaluate their letter spacing by comparing their words with the models. Guide children to recognize why one word might be better than another.

COACHING HINT

To accommodate the needs of children with various modality strengths, introduce letters in three steps:

1. Talk about the letter—its size, shape, and strokes. (auditory)
2. Demonstrate the letter on the chalkboard. (visual)
3. Have the children trace the letter in the air or on some other surface. (kinesthetic)

PRACTICE MASTER 19

Trace and write.

like   lid   lift   let   live

Write your own words.

Name

Copyright © Zaner-Bloser, Inc.   PRACTICE MASTER 19

PRACTICE MASTER 20

Trace and write.

L   L   L   L   L   L

Laura likes lemons.

Write a name that begins with L.

Name

Copyright © Zaner-Bloser, Inc.   PRACTICE MASTER 20

WRITING CORNER

Provide children with drawing paper to create "L staircases" using pull down straight and slide right strokes. (kinesthetic)

Draw rows of dots on paper or on the chalkboard. Invite the children to practice making straight lines with pull down or slide right strokes to connect the dots. When they add a line that makes a box, they can write the first letter of their name inside the box. (kinesthetic)

Touch the midline; pull down straight to the baseline. Lift. Dot.

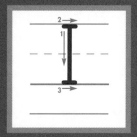

Touch the headline; pull down straight to the base-line. Lift. Touch the headline; slide right. Lift. Touch the baseline; slide right.

MODEL

Write **i** on guidelines as you say the stroke descriptions. Invite children to write **i** on their desks with their index fingers. Have them say the descriptions with you as they write. Follow the same procedure for **I**.

PRACTICE

Let children practice writing **i** and **I** on laminated writing cards or slates before they write on the pages.

Trace and write i.

Trace and write I.

Trace and write words with i.

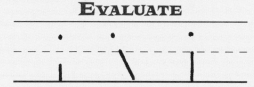
it   is   in

Trace and write names that begin with I.

Ivan   Iris

Circle your best i and I.

Write your name.
Is there an i or I in your name?   Yes   No

26

EVALUATE

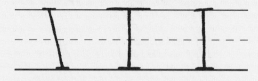

To help children evaluate their writing, ask questions such as these:
Does your **i** begin at the midline?
Is your letter straight up and down?
Is your **i** resting on the baseline?
Is your dot halfway between the headline and midline?

Are your strokes straight?
Is your letter straight up and down?
Is your **I** about the same width as the model?

BETTER LETTERS

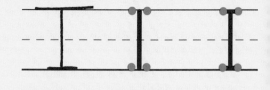

To help children write a vertical stroke, check the position of the paper and have them relax their hold on the pencil. Place a dot for *start* and a dot for *stop*. Say the descriptions as the children write **i**.

To help children write the slide right strokes of **I** the correct width, have them trace the pull down straight stroke and then connect dots placed at appropriate widths on the headline and baseline. Say the descriptions as they write **I**.

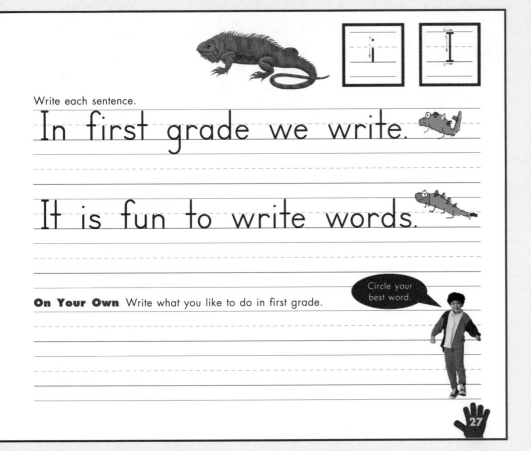

Write each sentence.

In first grade we write.

It is fun to write words.

On Your Own Write what you like to do in first grade.

Circle your best word.

27

FuN and GameS

I OR i GAME

Write **I** and **i** on the chalkboard. Have the children sit in a line facing the chalkboard. Write all the children's names on index cards and place them in a bag. Choose one and ask whose name it is. Identify any **i** in the name. Ask the child to trace either **I** or **i** on the board. If the child traces **I**, he or she demonstrates an action a person can do for classmates to imitate. If the child traces **i**, he or she makes up a riddle about an animal or object for classmates to guess. (visual, kinesthetic, auditory)

WRITING CORNER

Paste one row of guidelines at the top of drawing paper. Have the children write *I like* on the lines. Then invite them to draw pictures of things, food, animals, or people they like. Suggest they talk in pairs or cooperative groups about the pictures. Children may label their pictures. (visual)

I like birthdays.

WRITE SENTENCES

Before children write the two sentences on the page, ask them how they know where one word ends and another begins. Help them discover that the spaces between words are the same width. After children write, have them check to see that their spaces between words are about the same width. Have them use their index fingers to measure spaces between words. Guide children to recognize why one sentence might be better than another.

COACHING HINT

Demonstrate the correct way to hold a pencil. Right-handed teachers will better understand the left-handed child if they practice the left-handed position themselves. The Zaner-Bloser Writing Frame can help children achieve good hand position because the hand automatically settles into the correct position.

PRACTICE MASTER 21

Trace and write.

i i i i i i i i i i

in if ill into ice

Write your own words.

Name

Copyright © Zaner-Bloser, Inc.   PRACTICE MASTER 21

PRACTICE MASTER 22

Trace and write.

I I I I I I I I I I

Ike is eight now.

Write a name that begins with I

Name

Copyright © Zaner-Bloser, Inc.   PRACTICE MASTER 22

27

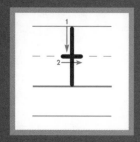

Touch the headline; pull down straight to the baseline. Lift. Touch the midline; slide right.

Touch the headline; pull down straight to the baseline. Lift. Touch the headline; slide right.

MODEL

Write t on guidelines as you say the stroke descriptions. Have groups of children come to the chalkboard, dip their index fingers in a container of water, and write t on the board. Have them say the descriptions with you as they write. Follow the same procedure for T.

PRACTICE

Let children practice writing t and T on laminated writing cards or slates before they write on the pages.

Trace and write t.

Trace and write T.

Trace and write words with t.

these   tell

Trace and write names that begin with T.

Tony   Terri

Write your name.
Is there a t or T in your name?   Yes   No

Circle your best t and T.

28

EVALUATE

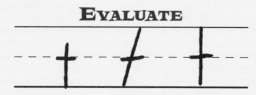

To help children evaluate their writing, ask questions such as these:
Does your t begin at the headline?
Does your t rest on the baseline?
Is your letter straight up and down?

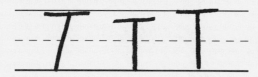

Are your strokes straight?
Is your letter straight up and down?
Is your slide right on the headline?
Is your T about the same width as the model?

BETTER LETTERS

To help children avoid slanting t, remind them to shift the paper as the writing progresses. Have them practice pulling their index fingers straight down from the headline to the baseline before writing.

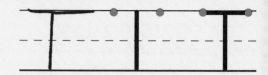

To help children determine the width of the slide right stroke, make the T's pull down straight stroke; then put dots on the headline for them to connect. Point out that the pull down straight stroke is midway on the slide right stroke.

Write each sentence.

These tapes tell stories.

I like to listen.

On Your Own Write what you like to listen to.

Circle your best word.

29

RHYME AND WRITE

Write three guidelines on the chalkboard. Write **s** on the first, **l** on the next, and **f** on the third. Then invite volunteers to write -*it* after each letter on the board. Explain that these words rhyme because they have the same ending letters. Read the rhyming words together. You may extend the activity using other letters, such as -*ill*, -*ip*, -*id*, and -*ix*. Help children determine which combinations make real words. (visual, auditory)

WRITE SENTENCES

Before children write the two sentences on the page, have them note the spaces between words as clues to show where one word ends and another begins. Invite children to count the number of words in each sentence. After they write their own sentences, have them work in pairs to check spacing between words and to count the words. Guide children to recognize why one sentence might be better than another.

COACHING HINT

If children's letters are not vertical, check to see if they need practice with any of the following: positioning the paper correctly, pulling the downstrokes in the proper direction, shifting the paper as the writing line fills.

PRACTICE MASTER 23

Trace and write.

t t t t t t t

top tree take to two

Write your own words.

Name

Copyright © Zaner-Bloser, Inc.   PRACTICE MASTER 23

PRACTICE MASTER 24

Trace and write.

T T T T T T T

Tess tells great tales.

Write a name that begins with T.

Name

Copyright © Zaner-Bloser, Inc.   PRACTICE MASTER 24

PHONICS CONNECTION

Have children prepare textured letters for a listening game. On tagboard or paper, have children write **t** and **T**. Have them glue small pieces of macaroni on the letters. Ask what letter begins the word *tiger*. Say some words that begin like *tiger* and some that do not. Ask children to listen as you say each word and to trace **t** only if the word you say begins like *tiger*. Extend the game by using people's names and uppercase **T**. (auditory, kinesthetic)

Touch below the midline; circle back (left) all the way around.

Touch below the headline; circle back (left) all the way around.

Note with the children that the differences in the two letters are the starting place and the size.

MODEL

Write **o** on guidelines as you say the stroke descriptions. Give each child a circular carton lid. Invite children to trace the outer edge of the lid with their fingers as you say the descriptions. Show them where to begin and in which direction to circle.

PRACTICE

Let children practice writing **o** and **O** on laminated writing cards or slates before they write on the pages.

Trace and write o.

Trace and write O.

Trace and write words with o.

of one

Trace and write names that begin with O.

Otto Ora

Write your name.
Is there an o or O in your name? Yes No

Circle your best o and O.

30

EVALUATE

To help children evaluate their writing, ask questions such as these:
Does your **o** rest on the baseline?
Is your **o** made with a backward circle stroke?
Is your **o** round?

Is your **O** round?
Does your **O** rest on the baseline?
Is your **O** closed properly?
Is your **O** about the same width as the model?

BETTER LETTERS

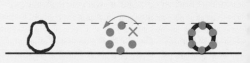

To help children make a round **o**, have them use a template or trace around tagboard circles. On paper, place a dot for *start* and several other dots to form a circle. Invite them to connect the dots by circling back (left) without lifting the pencil.

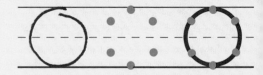

To help children close **O**, tell them to keep looking at the starting point while completing the circle. Using guidelines, place a few dots to help the children as they write while you say the stroke descriptions.

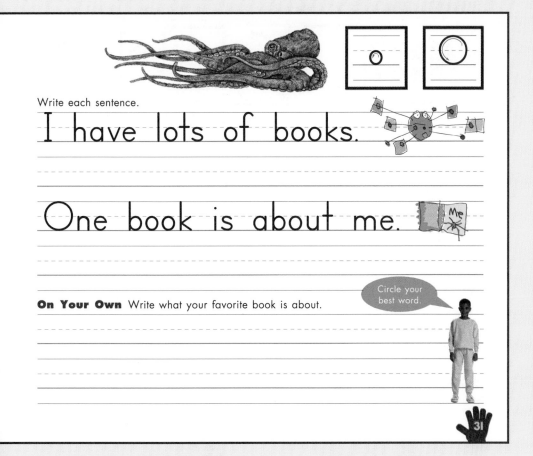

Write each sentence.

I have lots of books.

One book is about me.

On Your Own Write what your favorite book is about.

Circle your best word.

31

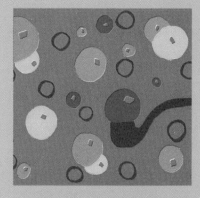
Oo COLLAGE

Have fun blowing bubbles with the children. Then make a Bubble O collage. Put a large sheet of paper, on which you have drawn a bubble pipe, on the floor and let children create bubbles. They can cut circular shapes from paper or fabric scraps and glue them to the collage. Cut handwriting paper into circles and have children write O and o on the guidelines. Have them add these bubbles to the collage. (visual, kinesthetic)

CIRCLE BACK GAME

To help children understand circle back, have them join hands and circle left as they sing these words to the tune of "In and Out the Window." (auditory, kinesthetic)

Circle back around
   the classroom
(Repeat twice more.)
And trace O in the air.

(Children stop and in the air trace O.)

Vary the last line with

Circle back to make an O.
My fingers make an O.

WRITE SENTENCES

Before the children write the two sentences on the page, write the word *books* using guidelines on the chalkboard, leaving large or uneven spaces between letters. Invite them to comment on whether this word is written correctly. Rewrite the word, pointing out that letters in a word should be spaced close to one another but not touching. After children write, have them compare their letter spacing with the models. Guide children to recognize why one word might be better than another.

COACHING HINT

Having children trace a set of sandpaper letters can provide kinesthetic reinforcement of letter formation. You can also provide auditory reinforcement if you or the children say the strokes as they trace the letters. (kinesthetic, auditory)

PRACTICE MASTER 25

Trace and write.

o o o o o o o

on off out our old

Write your own words.

Name

Copyright © Zaner-Bloser, Inc.   PRACTICE MASTER 25

PRACTICE MASTER 26

Trace and write.

O O O O O O

Omar won an orange.

Write a name that begins with O.

Name

Copyright © Zaner-Bloser, Inc.   PRACTICE MASTER 26

31

Touch below the midline; circle back (left) all the way around. Push up straight to the midline. Pull down straight to the baseline.

Touch the headline; slant left to the baseline. Lift. Touch the headline; slant right to the baseline. Lift. Touch the midline; slide right.

MODEL

Write **a** on guidelines as you say the stroke descriptions. Model writing **a** in the air as you repeat the descriptions. Have children echo them as they write **a** in the air with you. Follow the same procedure for **A**.

PRACTICE

Let children practice writing **a** and **A** on laminated writing cards or slates before they write on the pages.

Trace and write a.

Trace and write A.

Trace and write words with a.

Trace and write names that begin with A.

Write your name.
Is there an a or A in your name?   Yes   No

Circle your best a and A.

EVALUATE

To help children evaluate their writing, ask questions such as these:
Is your circle round?
Does your **a** touch the midline?

Are your strokes straight?
Is your slide right stroke on the midline?
Do your slant strokes touch the headline at the same spot?
Is your **A** about the same width as the model?

BETTER LETTERS

To help children write **a** without lifting the pencil, remind them not to lift the pencil from the paper after the circle back stroke but to go right into the push up stroke. Put three aligned dots as shown and refer to them as you give the stroke descriptions.

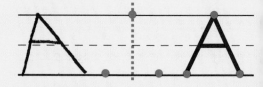

To help children write **A** the correct width, place two dots on the baseline and a dot on the headline as shown. Have them connect the dots with slant left and slant right lines and make a slide right line on the midline.

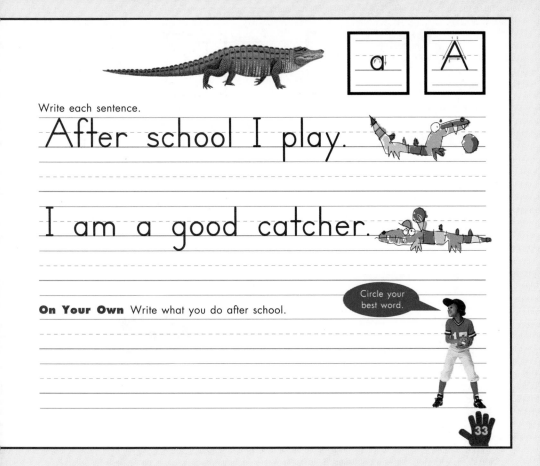

Write each sentence.

After school I play.

I am a good catcher.

On Your Own Write what you do after school.

Circle your best word.

33

Record letter names and stroke descriptions on an audiocassette tape. Use these letters: **A, a, O, o, T, t, I, i, L, l.** Provide a cassette player. Invite children to listen and write the letters following the descriptions on the tape. Make new cassette tapes as other letters are introduced. Later, make a game of the procedure by describing a letter for childen to write in the air. Have them call out the letter as they recognize it. (auditory, kinesthetic)

WRITE SENTENCES

Before children write the two sentences on the page, write the word *school* three ways: correctly spaced, spaced too far apart, and spaced too close together. Have them comment on the spacing in each word. After children write, have them work in pairs to comment on the spacing of letters in words their partners have written. Guide children to recognize why one word might be better than another.

PRACTICE MASTER 27

Trace and write.

a a a a a a a a a

all are ask ant any

Write your own words.

Name

Copyright © Zaner-Bloser, Inc.   PRACTICE MASTER 27

COACHING HINT

Children need to develop a clear mental image of the letter to be written. They should look at the letter first. To help them develop such an image, ask questions about the shape and size of the letter and the kinds of strokes used to form it. For **A**, children should note the slant lines and may form them by holding their two index fingers together in a slant. (visual)

PRACTICE MASTER 28

Trace and write.

A A A A A A A

Arnie ate the apples.

Write a name that begins with A.

Name

Copyright © Zaner-Bloser, Inc.   PRACTICE MASTER 28

PHONICS CONNECTION

Prepare a tray of wet sand or shaving cream on a table. Tell children to listen for words that begin with the first sound they hear in *alligator*. Then say words such as *ask, apple, dog, tree,* and *ax.* Tell children to write **a** in the sand or shaving cream if the word begins like *alligator.* Repeat with names of people and have children write **A.** (auditory, kinesthetic)

Touch below the midline; circle back (left) all the way around. Push up straight to the headline. Pull down straight to the baseline.

Touch the headline; pull down straight to the baseline. Lift. Touch the headline; slide right; curve forward (right) to the baseline; slide left.

MODEL

Write **d** on guidelines as you say the stroke descriptions. Have children trace the model **d** in their books as you repeat the descriptions. Follow the same procedure for **D**.

PRACTICE

Let children practice writing **d** and **D** on laminated writing cards or slates before they write on the pages.

34

Trace and write d.

Trace and write D.

Trace and write words with d.

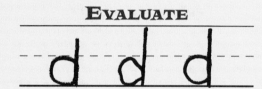
dog dream

Trace and write names that begin with D.

Dave Dina

Write your name.
Is there a d or D in your name?   Yes   No

Circle your best d and D.

34

EVALUATE

To help children evaluate their writing, ask questions such as these:
Does your **d** touch the headline?
Is your circle round?

Are your slide right and slide left strokes the same width?
Is your pull down straight stroke straight?
Does your **D** curve at the right place?

BETTER LETTERS

To help children make the pull down straight stroke touch the right side of the circle, place three dots as shown. Color the middle dot to show where the backward circle begins and ends. As the children write **d**, say the stroke descriptions and refer to the dots.

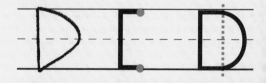

To help the children make the curved part of **D** correctly, stress that the slide right and the slide left strokes must be the same width. Write **D**; draw a dotted line between the slide lines as shown and have the children trace the curve to connect them.

Write each sentence.

I dreamed I had a dog.

Dreams can seem real.

On Your Own Write about one of your dreams.

Circle your best word.

35

CLAY LETTERS

Invite children to make the letters **d** and **D** from modeling clay. Then have them work in pairs, one saying the stroke descriptions and the other tracing the clay letters, first with eyes open and then closed. Have children reverse roles. They may want to make other letters or write their names with the clay. (kinesthetic)

ALPHABET BIG BOOK

Begin a class Alphabet Big Book, making a page for each letter children have learned. On guidelines at the top of a piece of tagboard, write the uppercase and lowercase letter, asking children to say the stroke descriptions with you as you write. Suggest that they work cooperatively to draw pictures whose names begin with the letter. Invite them to label each picture with its first letter. Bind pages together with rings. (visual)

WRITE SENTENCES

Before children write the two sentences on the page, call attention to the shape of the letters. Have them name and trace letters made with only straight lines, only a backward circle, and a combination of both. After children write, have them evaluate their letters made with a straight line and a backward circle by comparing them with the models. Guide children to recognize why one sentence might be better than another.

COACHING HINT

To help children develop familiarity with slide right and slide left strokes, invite them to practice the motion of sliding. Have children stand along a line of masking tape with their feet together facing you. Demonstrate how to slide right and slide left along the line. Have children demonstrate each slide as you name it. (kinesthetic)

PRACTICE MASTER 29

Trace and write.

d   d   d   d   d   d   d

day   down   door   dad

Write your own words.

Name

Copyright © Zaner-Bloser, Inc.   PRACTICE MASTER 29

PRACTICE MASTER 30

Trace and write.

D   D   D   D   D   D

Dina played her drums.

Write a name that begins with D.

Name

Copyright © Zaner-Bloser, Inc.   PRACTICE MASTER 30

Touch the headline; pull down straight to halfway between the midline and the baseline. Lift. Dot.

Touch below the headline; curve forward (right) to the midline; pull down straight to halfway between the midline and the baseline. Lift. Dot.

MODEL

Write ! on guidelines as you say the stroke descriptions. Model writing ! in the air as you repeat the descriptions. Have children echo them as they write !'s in the air with you. Follow the same procedure for ?

PRACTICE

Let children practice writing ! and ? on laminated writing cards or slates before they write on the pages.

Trace and write !.

Trace and write ?.

Trace and write an exclamation.

Surprise!

Trace and write a question.

Who?

Circle your best ! and ?.

Write your name.

36

EVALUATE

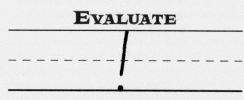

To help children evaluate their writing, ask questions such as these:
Does your exclamation point begin at the headline?
Is your pull down straight stroke straight up and down?
Does your dot rest on the baseline directly under the pull down straight stroke?

Is your question mark about the same width as the model?
Does it begin with a curve forward and end with a pull down straight stroke?
Does it have a dot on the baseline?

BETTER LETTERS

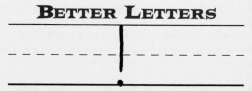

To help children write a vertical ! with the dot correctly aligned, have them practice pulling their index fingers straight down from the headline to halfway between the midline and the baseline, lifting and making a dot on the baseline under the stroke. Say the descriptions as the children write !

To help children write ? the correct width, place a green and a red dot for the start and the end of the curve. Have children make the curve. Show them how to make a pull down straight stroke, lift and add a dot correctly aligned.

Write each sentence.

Knock! Knock!

Who is there?

Put a ☺ next to your best sentence.

On Your Own Write an answer.

MOBILES: ! AND ?

Draw exclamation points and question marks on card stock or construction paper. Ask children to cut these out and add designs. Attach the dot. Then have them write either a question or an exclamation on an index card with guidelines. Attach the card and hang the mobile. Invite children to share their exclamations and questions with classmates. (visual)

WRITING CORNER

Write statements, questions, and exclamations, but do not include punctuation marks. The following may serve as models:

Stop
I am here
Did Tim fall

After children read a sentence, have them write it and add the appropriate end mark. (visual)

WRITE SENTENCES

Before children write the sentences on the page, call attention to the space between the last letter in the word and the exclamation point or question mark. Point out that this is the same amount of space as between letters. After children write, have them evaluate their spacing and formation of end marks by comparing their words with the models. Guide them to recognize why one sentence might be better than another.

COACHING HINT

Make ! and ? from beans or sandpaper. Children who are having difficulty forming these punctuation marks can trace the tactile versions several times with their fingers and then practice writing each end mark on the chalkboard. (kinesthetic)

To make a larger writing space for those who need it, fold a sheet of unlined paper lengthwise. Three guidelines will be formed, the midline being the fold. (visual, kinesthetic)

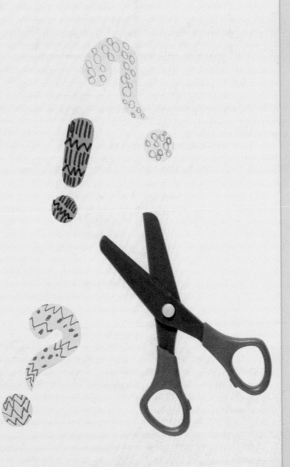

On guidelines on the chalk-board write **IL**, **iI**, **tT**, **oO**, **aA**, and **dD.** Have children take turns naming the letter pairs and pointing to each uppercase and lowercase letter.

Call attention to the size and shape of letters by asking questions such as these: Which letters are tall? Which letters are short? Which letters begin with a pull down straight stroke? Which letters begin with a circle back stroke?

MODEL

Write **IL** on guidelines as you say the stroke descriptions for each letter. Model writing the letters in the air as you repeat the descriptions. Have children echo them as they write the letters in the air with you. Follow the same procedure for **iI**, **tT**, **oO**, **aA**, and **dD.**

PRACTICE

Let children practice writing the letter pairs **IL**, **iI**, **tT**, **oO**, **aA**, and **dD** on laminated writing cards or slates before they write on the pages.

38

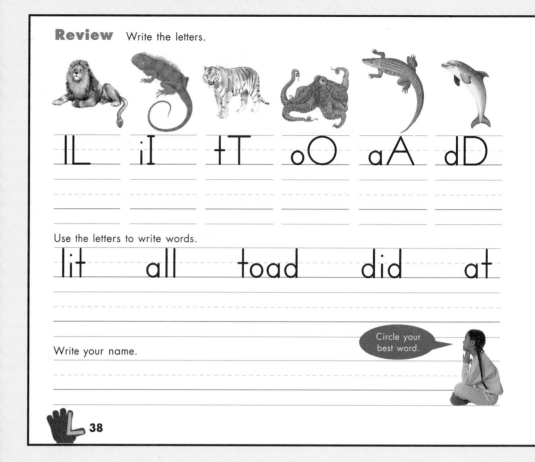

Review Write the letters.

IL   iI   tT   oO   aA   dD

Use the letters to write words.

lit   all   toad   did   at

Write your name.

Circle your best word.

38

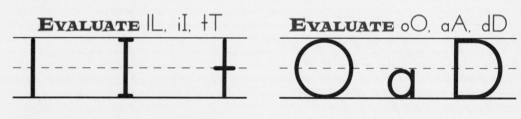

EVALUATE IL, iI, tT

I I t

To help children evaluate their writing, ask questions such as these:
Is your **I** straight up and down?
Does your **L** touch the headline and base-line?
Does your **i** begin at the midline?
Is your **I** about the same width as the model?
Is the slide right stroke of your **t** on the midline?
Are the strokes in your **T** straight?

EVALUATE oO, aA, dD

O a D

To help children evaluate their writing, ask question such as these:

Are your backward circles round in **o** and **O**?
Do your **o** and **O** look alike except for size?
Does **a** end at the baseline?
Are your slant strokes in **A** straight?
Does your **d** have a round backward circle?
Is your **D** about the same width as the model?

Write the sentences.

Off we go. Toot!

Are we there yet?

Look! I see the ocean.

My Words

Put a 😊 next to your best sentence.

39

WRITE SENTENCES

Before children write the sentences on the page, call attention to the spacing between the sentences on the first line. Note that the space after the period is wider than the space between words. Ask how many sentences they see. After they write, have them compare their spacing with the models. Guide children to recognize why one sentence might be better than another.

MY WORDS

Ask children to write words of their own. Encourage them to write words that contain the review letters. If they need help, suggest they look for words on the previous pages.

COACHING HINT

Remind children that there is a wider space between sentences than between words. Show them how to place two fingers between sentences and one finger between words. (kinesthetic)

STORY STARTER

Display the story starter *Look! I see _____.* Have children write it on paper and complete the sentence. Then ask them to cut out the completed sentence, attach it to drawing paper, and illustrate it. As children share their writing, ask classmates to add ideas to continue each story orally. (visual, kinesthetic, auditory)

Look! I see a house.

Touch below the midline; circle back (left), ending above the baseline.

Touch below the headline; circle back (left), ending above the baseline.

MODEL

Write **c** on guidelines as you say the stroke descriptions. Model writing **c** in the air as you repeat the descriptions. Have children echo them as they write **c** in the air with you. Follow the same procedure for **C**.

PRACTICE

Let children practice writing **c** and **C** on laminated writing cards or slates before they write on the pages.

Trace and write c.

c c c c c

Trace and write C.

C C C C

Trace and write words with c.

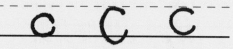

can cats

Trace and write names that begin with C.

Coco Cal

Write your name.
Is there a c or C in your name?   Yes   No

Circle your best c and C.

40

EVALUATE

c c c

To help children evaluate their writing, ask questions such as these:
Does your **c** look like a circle that has not been closed?
Does your **c** start a little below the midline?
Does your **c** stop a little above the baseline?

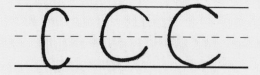

C C C

Is your **C** about the same width as the model?
Does your **C** rest on the baseline?

BETTER LETTERS

C C C

To help children begin and end **c** correctly, draw a vertical line and on this line, place a dot for *start* just below the midline and a dot for *stop* just above the baseline. Show them how to make a backward circle stroke between the two dots to form **c.**

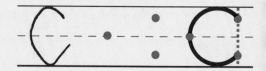

To help children begin and end **C** correctly, make three dots representing the beginning, middle, and end of the letter. Invite them to write the letter using the dots as a guide. Check alignment by drawing a vertical line between beginning and end dots.

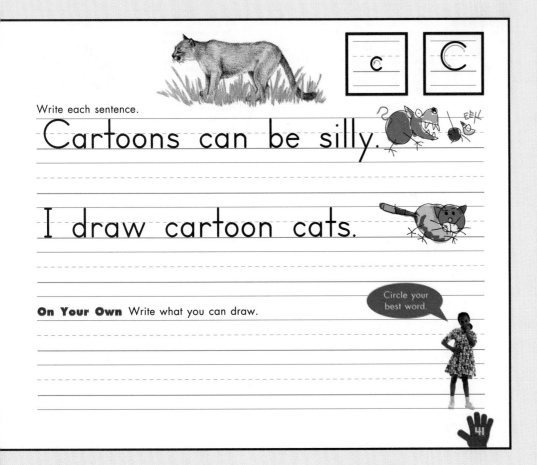

Write each sentence.

Cartoons can be silly.

I draw cartoon cats.

On Your Own Write what you can draw.

Circle your best word.

41

WRITING CORNER

Show children how to draw a cat using only **c**'s. Invite them to draw their own cat using c's and label it. Children may enjoy using other letters as the basis for creating more animal pictures. (visual)

PHONICS CONNECTION

Play this hand-clap game until children are able to chant with you.

All: Who took the cookie from the cookie jar?

Teacher: Carol took the cookie from the cookie jar.

Carol: Who, me?

Teacher: Yes, you.

Carol: Couldn't be.

Teacher: Then who?

Carol: Sam took the cookie from the cookie jar.

Have each child write **Cc** on a brown paper circle (cookie). Invite children to think of words that begin with /k/ as in *cookie*. When a child names a word, he or she can place the cookie on a bulletin board cookie jar. (auditory)

WRITE SENTENCES

Before children write the two sentences on the page, help them notice that the letters in these sentences are straight up and down. After they write, have them evaluate whether or not their letters stand straight. Point out that an uppercase letter is used to begin a sentence. Guide children to recognize why one sentence might be better than another.

COACHING HINT

To help children with the backward circle, make a large circle on the floor with tape. Ask the children to walk, hop, or jump around the circle in a counter-clockwise direction. (kinesthetic)

PRACTICE MASTER 31

Trace and write.

C C C C C C C C

car   cow   city   class

Write your own words.

Name

Copyright © Zaner-Bloser, Inc.   PRACTICE MASTER 31

PRACTICE MASTER 32

Trace and write.

C C C C C C C

Cindy picked the carrots.

Write a name that begins with C.

Name

Copyright © Zaner-Bloser, Inc.   PRACTICE MASTER 32

Touch halfway between the midline and baseline; slide right; circle back (left), ending above the baseline.

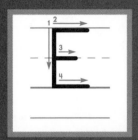

Touch the headline; pull down straight to the baseline. Lift. Touch the headline; slide right. Lift. Touch the midline; slide right. Stop short. Lift. Touch the baseline; slide right.

MODEL

Write e on guidelines as you say the stroke descriptions. Invite children to use their index fingers to write e's on their desks as you repeat the descriptions and they echo them. Follow the same procedure for E.

PRACTICE

Let children practice writing e and E on laminated writing cards or slates before they write on the pages.

42

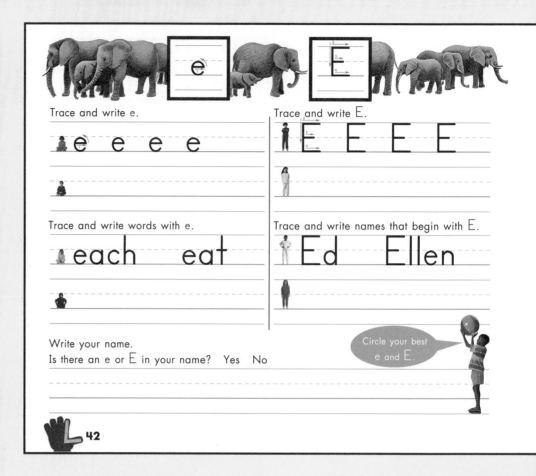

Trace and write e.

Trace and write E.

Trace and write words with e.

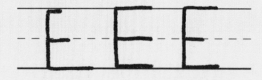

Trace and write names that begin with E.

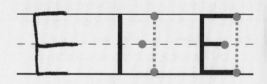

Write your name.
Is there an e or E in your name?   Yes   No

Circle your best e and E.

42

EVALUATE

To help children evaluate their writing, ask questions such as these:
Is your slide right stroke straight?
Is your backward circle open?
Does your e look round?

Are your top and bottom slide right strokes the same width?
Is your middle slide right stroke shorter than the other two?
Is your E about the same width as the model?

BETTER LETTERS

To help children touch the slide right stroke of e when circling back, place a dot where the slide right starts and a dot where it ends. Demonstrate how to connect the dots for the slide right and circle back touching the beginning dot.

To help children make E the correct width, have them make a pull down straight stroke. Add three dots to show where the slide right lines should end. Have them complete E. Draw a vertical dotted line to show which slide right lines align.

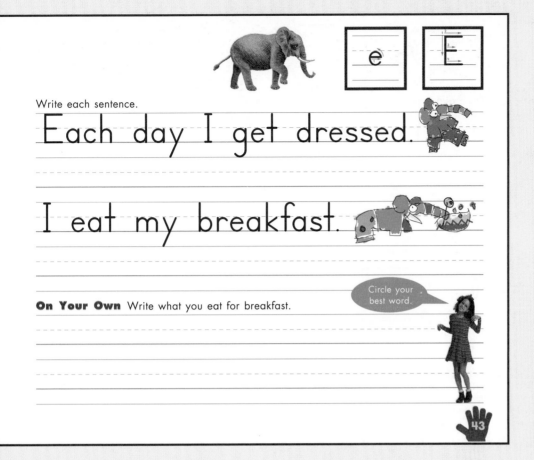

Write each sentence.

Each day I get dressed.

I eat my breakfast.

On Your Own Write what you eat for breakfast.

Circle your best word.

43

elephant

egg

PHONICS CONNECTION

Write *echo* on the chalkboard and demonstrate an echo by asking a child to repeat words after you. Tell children that *echo* begins with e. Then say words that begin like *echo (egg, exit, elephant, edge, every)* and have children echo you. Add words that begin with other sounds. They should echo only those words that begin like *echo*. (auditory)

RHYME AND WRITE

Introduce children to rhyming words with e. Write the following word groups on guidelines on the chalkboard: *bed, red, led; net, pet, set; ten, hen, men; see, bee, tree.* Read each group with the children. Then ask a question about one of the words, for example, "Which word names something to sleep on?" Have a child point to the word that answers the question and trace over the e with colored chalk. (auditory)

WRITE SENTENCES

Before children write the sentences on the page, review the basic strokes they have learned. Have them name a letter and tell what strokes are used to make it. After writing, have them compare the shape of their letters with the models. Guide children to recognize why one sentence might be better than another.

COACHING HINT

Help children practice using the term *halfway* and locating the halfway point between two lines. Make two parallel lines on the floor using masking tape. Have children take turns jumping to the halfway point between the lines. (visual)

PRACTICE MASTER 33

Trace and write.

e e e e e e e e

end eye even every

Write your own words.

Name

Copyright © Zaner-Bloser, Inc.   PRACTICE MASTER 33

PRACTICE MASTER 34

Trace and write.

E E E E E E E E

Evan eats scrambled eggs.

Write a name that begins with E.

Name

Copyright © Zaner-Bloser, Inc.   PRACTICE MASTER 34

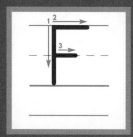

Touch below the headline; curve back (left); pull down straight to the baseline. Lift. Touch the midline; slide right.

Touch the headline; pull down straight to the baseline. Lift. Touch the headline; slide right. Lift. Touch the midline; slide right. Stop short.

MODEL

Write **f** on guidelines as you say the stroke descriptions. Model writing **f** in the air as you repeat the descriptions. Have children echo them as they write **f** in the air with you. Follow the same procedure for **F**.

PRACTICE

Let children practice writing **f** and **F** on laminated writing cards or slates before they write on the pages.

Trace and write f.

Trace and write F.

Trace and write words with f.

faces   fun

Trace and write names that begin with F.

Fred Faye

Write your name.
Is there an f or F in your name?   Yes   No

Circle your best f and F.

EVALUATE

To help children evaluate their writing, ask questions such as these:
Does your **f** begin below the headline?
Does your **f** rest on the baseline?
Is your slide right on the midline?

Are your strokes straight?
Is your letter straight up and down?
Does your second slide right line stop short?
Is your **F** about the same width as the model?

BETTER LETTERS

To help children write an **f** that begins with a curve back (left) stroke, place a green dot to show where the curve begins and another colored dot to show where the curve turns into a straight line. Say the stroke descriptions as they write **f**.

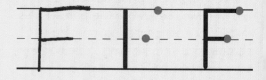

To help children write the slide right strokes of **F** the correct width, have them first write the pull down stroke. Place dots to indicate where the slide right strokes should end. Have them complete **F** as you say the stroke descriptions.

Write each sentence.

I can make fish faces.

Fish faces are fun.

On Your Own Write about a funny thing you do.

Circle your best word.

45

FISH FUN

Cover a bulletin board with blue paper. Have children use a sponge to paint drawing paper with different colors. When the paper is dry, help them draw and cut out large fish shapes. Trim paper and attach it to the fish. Have children label the fish with **f** and **F**. Place fish on the blue paper to create a sea scene. (visual, kinesthetic)

PHONICS CONNECTION

Say this **F** tongue twister for the children. Then have them say it slowly, then quickly, with you: *Fran fed Fred's frog.* Explain that in a tongue twister, the same sound is repeated in most words. Have children make up their own **F** tongue twisters. Then have them write **f** or **F** on lined paper. Say the tongue twisters and ask children to point to **f** or **F** each time they hear /f/. (auditory, visual)

WRITE SENTENCES

Before children write the two sentences on the page, have them share what they know about spacing between words in a sentence and between letters in a word. After children write, have them evaluate their spacing by comparing it to the models. Guide children to recognize why one sentence might be better than another.

COACHING HINT

Help children practice using the term *below* and locating the position. Distribute stickers or gummed stars and drawing paper. Help them draw a horizontal line across the page. Then direct them to place a sticker *on* the line, *just below* the line, and *just above* the line. Ask them to locate and circle the sticker that is just below the line. (auditory, kinesthetic)

PRACTICE MASTER 35

Trace and write.

f f f f f f f f

fish fix fire fast for

Write your own words.

Name

Copyright © Zaner-Bloser, Inc.   PRACTICE MASTER 35

PRACTICE MASTER 36

Trace and write.

F F F F F F

Fiona fishes for fun.

Write a name that begins with F.

Name

Copyright © Zaner-Bloser, Inc.   PRACTICE MASTER 36

CONTINUOUS STROKE

Touch below the midline; circle back (left) all the way around. Push up straight to the midline. Pull down straight through the baseline; curve back (left).

Touch below the headline; circle back (left), ending at the midline. Slide left.

MODEL

Write **g** on guidelines as you say the stroke descriptions. Invite several children to dip a small sponge in water and use it to write **g** on the chalkboard while others say the descriptions with you. Follow the same procedure for **G**.

PRACTICE

Let children practice writing **g** and **G** on laminated writing cards or slates before they write on the page.

46

Trace and write g.

Trace and write G.

Trace and write words with g.

guess   got

Trace and write names that begin with G.

Gina   Gus

Write your name.
Is there a g or G in your name?   Yes   No

Circle your best g and G.

46

EVALUATE

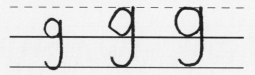

To help children evaluate their writing, ask questions such as these:
Does your **g** start below the midline?
Is your **g** made with a backward circle stroke?
Does your **g** end below the baseline?

Does your **G** begin below the headline?
Is your slide left on the midline?
Is your **G** about the same width as the model?

BETTER LETTERS

To help children make the descending line correctly, demonstrate how to pull down straight through the baseline and where to begin the small curve that rests on the next headline and turns up. Say the stroke descriptions as the children write **g**.

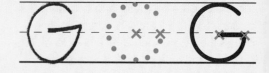

To help children start and end the slide left stroke of **G** correctly, dot around a backward circle and place two **x**'s on the midline as shown. Demonstrate how to stop before making the slide left stroke on the midline. Have children trace your **G**.

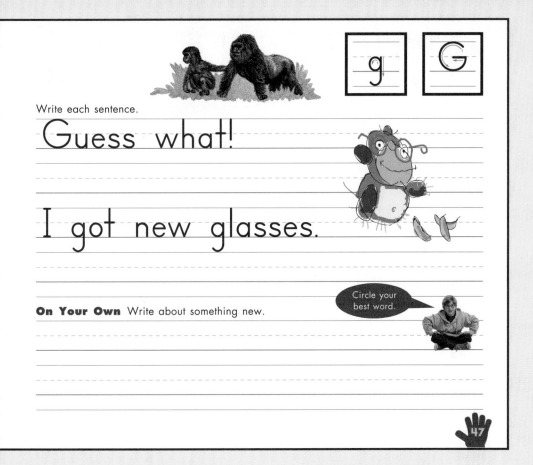

Write each sentence.

Guess what!

I got new glasses.

On Your Own Write about something new.

Circle your best word.

47

SHAPE AND TRACE LETTERS

In a shoe box, place pieces of yarn or string, pipe cleaners, craft sticks, paper strips and circles, and cotton swabs. Invite children to work in pairs. Have them use the materials to form **g** and **G**. Then have partners take turns saying descriptions and tracing the letters. (kinesthetic, auditory)

GIGANTIC, GLITTERY g AND G

Write oversized **g** and **G** on a large sheet of paper. Invite children to add glue and glitter to the letters. Display them on a bulletin board. Ask children to help you make a list of words that have the same beginning sound as *gorilla*. Use riddles to help them. Then have each child write one of those words on lined paper, cut it out, and paste it near the glittery letters. (visual, auditory)

WRITE SENTENCES

Before children write the two sentences on the page, write words from the second sentence in mixed-up order using guidelines on the chalkboard. Have children suggest a sentence and take turns writing the words. Call attention to the space between words. After children write, have them compare their spacing with the models. Guide children to recognize why one sentence might be better than another.

COACHING HINT

Correct paper placement is a critical factor in legibility. To assure that the paper is placed correctly, for both right- and left-handed children, use tape to form a frame on the desk so the children will be able to place the paper in the correct position. (visual)

PRACTICE MASTER 37

Trace and write.

g g g g g g g g

girl grow good game

Write your own words.

Name

Copyright © Zaner-Bloser, Inc.　　PRACTICE MASTER 37

PRACTICE MASTER 38

Trace and write.

G G G G G G

Gail ate green grapes.

Write a name that begins with G.

Name

Copyright © Zaner-Bloser, Inc.　　PRACTICE MASTER 38

Touch the midline; pull down straight through the baseline; curve back (left). Lift. Dot.

Touch the headline; pull down straight; curve back (left). Lift. Touch the headline; slide right.

MODEL

Write **j** on guidelines as you say the stroke descriptions. Invite children to use an index finger to write **j** on their desks. Have them say the descriptions with you as they write. Follow the same procedure for **J**.

PRACTICE

Let children practice writing **j** and **J** on laminated writing cards or slates before they write on the pages.

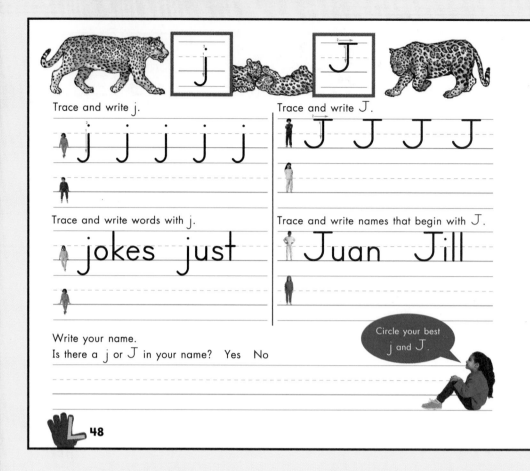

Trace and write j.

Trace and write J.

Trace and write words with j.

jokes   just

Trace and write names that begin with J.

Juan   Jill

Write your name.
Is there a j or J in your name?   Yes   No

Circle your best j and J.

48

EVALUATE

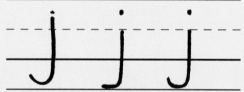

To help children evaluate their writing, ask questions such as these:
Does your **j** begin at the midline?
Is the bottom of your **j** round?
Is your dot halfway between the headline and midline?

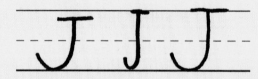

Does your **J** begin at the headline?
Is your slide right on the headline?
Is your **J** about the same width as the model?

BETTER LETTERS

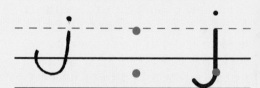

To help children begin the curve of **j** in the right place, demonstrate how to make the curve, starting between the baseline and the next writing line. Mark this spot with a dot as children write **j**, turning from a straight line into a curve.

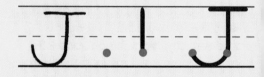

To help children write the curve of **J**, make several vertical lines ending above the baseline and then have children add the curve, which should touch the baseline and end about halfway to the midline.

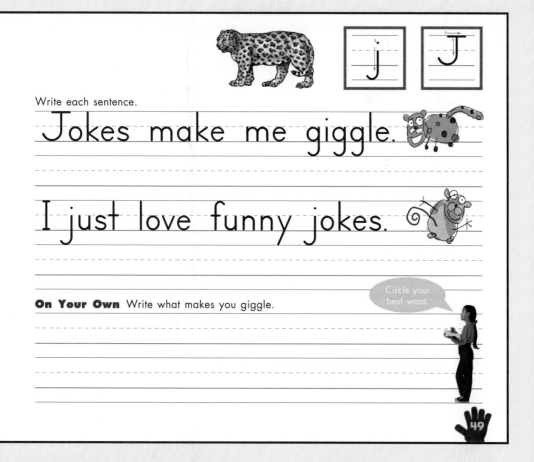

Write each sentence.

Jokes make me giggle.

I just love funny jokes.

On Your Own Write what makes you giggle.

Circle your best word.

49

LETTER JUMP

With chalk, draw a large **j** and **J** on the playground. Invite children to jump along the outline of the letter as you say directions for forming it. Then have children hop, walk, or tiptoe along the letter. Repeat the procedure with other letters. (kinesthetic)

WRITE SENTENCES

Before children write the two sentences on the page, have them compare the formation of the letters **g** and **j** and **o** and **e** in the words *jokes* and *giggle*. Note similarities in size, shape, and placement. After children write, have them compare their **g, j, o,** and **e** with the models. Guide children to recognize why one letter might be better than another.

COACHING HINT

To call attention to the part of a letter that descends below the baseline, write **g** and **j** on guidelines on the chalkboard. Have children trace the descending stroke with colored chalk to highlight its shape. (visual)

PRACTICE MASTER 39

Trace and write.

j j j j j j j

jet jog jar job join

Write your own words.

Name

Copyright © Zaner-Bloser, Inc.   PRACTICE MASTER 39

PRACTICE MASTER 40

Trace and write.

J J J J J J

Juana just jumped up.

Write a name that begins with J.

Name

Copyright © Zaner-Bloser, Inc.   PRACTICE MASTER 40

PHONICS CONNECTION

Write guidelines on the chalkboard. After everyone agrees that *jump* begins with **j**, ask the children to jump up every time they hear a word that begins like *jump*. Say other words, some that begin with **j**. Have a child write **j** on the chalkboard if the word begins with **j**. (auditory, kinesthetic)

ALPHABET BIG BOOK

Invite children to update the class Alphabet Big Book by adding pages with labeled drawings for new letters. (visual, auditory)

Touch below the midline; circle back (left) all the way around. Push up straight to the midline. Pull down straight through the baseline; curve forward (right).

Touch below the headline; circle back (left) all the way around. Lift. Slant right to the baseline.

MODEL

Write **q** on guidelines as you say the stroke descriptions. Model writing **q** on sandpaper. Pair children and have them take turns writing and saying descriptions. Follow the same procedure for **Q**.

PRACTICE

Let children practice writing **q** and **Q** on laminated writing cards or slates before they write on the pages.

Trace and write q.

Trace and write Q.

Trace and write words with q.

quit quack

Trace and write names that begin with Q.

Quito Quin

Circle your best q and Q.

Write your name.
Is there a q or Q in your name?   Yes   No

50

EVALUATE

To help children evaluate their writing, ask questions such as these:
Does your **q** begin below the midline?
Is your **q** made with a backward circle stroke?
Does your **q** touch the headline of the writing space below?

Does your **Q** look like an **O** except for the slant right stroke?
Does your slant right end on the baseline?

BETTER LETTERS

To help children become aware of continuous strokes in **q**, write **q** three times, each time highlighting a different stroke with a broken line. Invite children to trace each letter as you say stroke descriptions. Point out that the curve forward stroke is the bottom of a circle. Demonstrate how **q** differs from **g**.

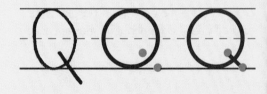

To help children with the placement and length of the slant right stroke in **Q**, have them write an **O**. Then put dots to show the start and end of the slant right line.

Write each sentence.

Quiet! Listen to me.

I quack like a duck.

On Your Own Write what animal noise you can make.

Circle your best word.

51

WRITE SENTENCES

Before children write on the page, write the following on guidelines on the chalkboard: *Quiet! Listen to me.* Ask which sentence has one word and which end mark is used. Ask where the first sentence ends and the second begins. Point out that there is more space between two sentences than between words within a sentence. After children write, have them compare their spacing with the models. Guide children to recognize why one sentence might be better than another.

COACHING HINT

Some children may confuse the letters **g** and **q.** Provide pipe cleaners so they can make the letter **g** and then follow its shape with their fingers. Ask them to write **g** on their paper three times and circle the best one. Follow the same procedure for **q.** (visual, kinesthetic)

PRACTICE MASTER 41

Trace and write.

q q q q q q q

quiz quilt quite quit

Write your own words.

Name

Copyright © Zaner-Bloser, Inc.   PRACTICE MASTER 41

PRACTICE MASTER 42

Trace and write.

Q Q Q Q Q Q

Quincy quit the game.

Write a name that begins with Q.

Name

Copyright © Zaner-Bloser, Inc.   PRACTICE MASTER 42

A LETTER QUILT

Ask for donations of cotton cloth and cut it into 3" squares. Attach the cloth squares to 5" squares of paper. Assign children a previously learned letter of the alphabet to write on the square, one uppercase and one lowercase. Arrange the squares on a bulletin board to form a quilt. Add children's names written in their own handwriting. (visual)

51

On guidelines on the chalkboard write **cC**, **eE**, **fF**, **gG**, **jJ**, and **qQ**. Have children take turns naming the letter pairs and pointing to each uppercase and lowercase letter.

Call attention to the size and shape of letters by asking questions such as these: Which short letters go below the baseline? Which letters begin with a circle back stroke? Which letters begin with a pull down straight stroke? Which two letters look alike except for their size?

MODEL

Write **cC** on guidelines as you say the stroke descriptions for each letter. Model writing the letters in the air as you repeat the descriptions. Have children echo them as they write the letters in the air with you. Follow the same procedure for **eE**, **fF**, **gG**, **jJ**, and **qQ**.

PRACTICE

Let children practice writing the letter pairs **cC**, **eE**, **fF**, **gG**, **jJ**, and **qQ** on laminated writing cards or slates before they write on the pages.

Review Write the letters.

cC   eE   fF   gG   jJ   qQ

Use the letters to write words.

cage   jog   quit   face

Circle your best word.

Write your name.

52

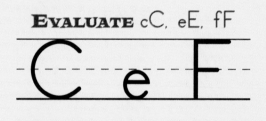

EVALUATE cC, eE, fF

C e F

To help children evaluate their writing, ask questions such as these:
Are your backward circles round in **c** and **C**?
Is the slide right stroke in your **e** straight?
Does your **E** touch the headline and baseline?
Does your **f** begin below the headline?
In **E** and **F,** is your second slide right stroke shorter than the first slide right stroke?

EVALUATE gG, jJ, qQ

g J q

To help children evaluate their writing, ask questions such as these:
Does your **g** go below the baseline and touch the next headline?
Does your **G** end with a slide left stroke?
Did you remember to dot your **j**?
Is your **J** about the same width as the model?
Does your **q** touch the next headline?
Is your slant stroke for **Q** correctly placed?

Write the sentences.

Join the race.

Get ready. Get set. Go.

Jump as fast as you can.

My Words

Put a ☺ next to your best sentence.

53

Write **A**way

READY, SET, GO

Encourage children to share their experiences watching or participating in races. Ask them to imagine a race between cars, bicycles, or other vehicles. Invite several children to describe the race they imagined. Have them illustrate their ideas and write a story to accompany their pictures. (auditory, visual, kinesthetic)

WRITE SENTENCES

Before children write the sentences, call attention to letter spacing in the words. Choose one word and write it on the chalkboard three times—once with letters too far apart, once correctly spaced, and once too close together. Have a volunteer choose which is correct and explain why. After children write, have them compare their letter spacing with the models. Guide them to recognize why one sentence might be better than another.

COACHING HINT

Using tape or chalk, make three guidelines a short distance apart on the floor. Invite children to take turns walking letters as you say the stroke descriptions for each letter. Select volunteers to write each letter on the board. (kinesthetic)

MY WORDS

Ask children to write words of their own. Encourage them to write words that contain the review letters. If they need help, suggest they look for words on the previous pages.

crab

CREEP OR CRAWL

Ask children to list words that tell how animals move. Ask them to draw a picture showing an animal in action and then label it with the animal's name and an action word. Encourage them to write stories about the animals pictured. (auditory, visual)

Review with children that letters are used to make words, words can be put together to make sentences, and sentences can go together to create a story. Call attention to the words on the page. Ask volunteers to read them aloud.

Tell children to write their own words or the words shown on the page. Provide materials for children to use as word sources.

PRACTICE

Let children practice writing words on laminated writing cards or slates before they write on the pages.

Evaluation
Show What You Can Do
Here are words I can write.

Write your name.

ate   toad
cat   goat
dog   quiet
jet   little
the

feet

Circle your best word.

54

EVALUATE

To help children evaluate their writing, ask questions such as these:

Are all your letters straight up and down?
Are all the letters in your words correctly spaced?
Are your tall letters written between the headline and baseline?
Do your short letters begin at the midline or below it?
Do letters that go below the baseline touch the headline below?
Did you dot your **i** and **j**?

Encourage children to share their work with a peer and to have their partner circle the word he or she thinks is best.

Certificates of Progress *should be awarded to those children who show notable hand-writing progress and* Certificates of Excellence *to those who progress to the top levels of handwriting proficiency.*

I can draw a picture.

I can write a story about my picture.

Put a 😊 next to your best sentence.

STORY STARTERS

To give children practice in writing sentences, have them complete sentence starters. Accept invented spellings. Ideas for sentence starters include the following:

I wish I had a pet _____ because _____.

When I play with friends, we _____.

Once upon a time I met a giant and _____.

One day two elephants _____.

Invite children to share their completed stories. (visual)

WRITE SENTENCES

Before children write, encourage a lively sharing of ideas about the different subjects they might choose for their pictures and story writing. You might list their suggestions on the chalkboard.

Encourage children to use several sentences to tell about their pictures. Remind them to begin each sentence with an uppercase letter and to include an end mark. Point out that they may find it helpful to use some of the words they wrote on the previous page.

After they write, have children check the spacing between words and sentences. Guide them to see why one sentence might be better than another.

Ask children to share their pictures and stories.

COACHING HINT

To reinforce correct word and sentence spacing, write two simple related sentences on lined paper, glue the paper to oak tag, and laminate it. Have children trace the sentences with a crayon. Guide the children to leave one finger space between words and two finger spaces between sentences. (kinesthetic)

ANIMAL RIDDLES

On the chalkboard, write *Who am I?* Tell children they will write riddles about different animals. Prepare index cards with animal names or pictures, and place them in a bag. Let each child take a card and write a description of the animal without naming it. Have the children complete their riddles with the question from the chalkboard. Invite them to share and answer the riddles. (visual)

Touch the midline; pull down straight; curve forward (right); push up to the midline. Pull down straight to the baseline.

Touch the headline; pull down straight; curve forward (right); push up to the headline.

MODEL

Write **u** on guidelines as you say the stroke descriptions. Invite children to use an index finger to write **u** on their desks. Have them say the descriptions with you as they write. Follow the same procedure for **U**.

PRACTICE

Let children practice writing **u** and **U** on laminated writing cards or slates before they write on the pages.

Trace and write u.

Trace and write U.

Trace and write words with u.

use   under

Trace and write names that begin with U.

Uri Una

Write your name.
Is there a u or U in your name?   Yes   No

Circle your best u and U.

56

EVALUATE

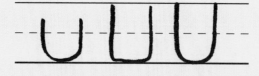

To help children evaluate their writing, ask questions such as these:
Are your pull down strokes straight?
Does the curve of your **u** rest on the baseline?

Does your **U** begin at the headline?
Is the curve of your **U** round?
Is your **U** about the same width as the model?

BETTER LETTERS

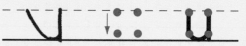

To help children make **u** vertical and the correct width, demonstrate the formation of **u**. Remind them to begin the letter with a pull down straight stroke. Point out where the forward curve begins and ends and how it connects smoothly to the push up stroke.

To help children begin and end the curve correctly, draw a dotted line across **U** to show where the curve forward stroke begins and ends. Have children trace the letter.

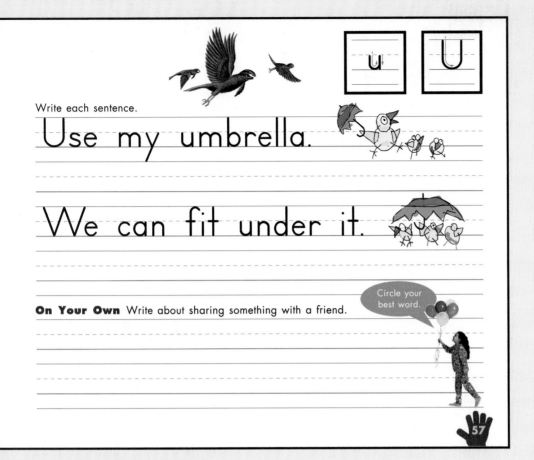

Write each sentence.

Use my umbrella.

We can fit under it.

On Your Own Write about sharing something with a friend.

Circle your best word.

57

TIC-TAC-U

Fold lined paper into four boxes and write a tic-tac-toe grid in each. Pair children and ask them to use **u** and **U** to play the game, instead of **X** and **O**. Suggest that each child use a different color to write. Children will play this game in the traditional way, trying to complete a vertical, horizontal, or diagonal row to win. (visual)

WRITING CORNER

If you previously prepared an audiotape with stroke descriptions, update it now for the new letters you have introduced. Invite children to listen to the descriptions on the audiotape and to write the letters on lined paper. To vary the activity, children might enjoy listening and then writing the letters in a layer of smooth, wet sand. (auditory, kinesthetic)

WRITE SENTENCES

Before children write the two sentences on the page, call attention to the spaces between words. Ask them to think of something that would fit into one space (a paper clip, a finger, a pencil). After children write, have them evaluate their spacing by using the measuring tool they selected. Guide children to recognize why one sentence might be better than another.

COACHING HINT

Using guidelines on the chalkboard, write a line of lowercase and uppercase letters with several obvious errors. Have children take turns correcting errors at the chalkboard. (visual)

PRACTICE MASTER 43

Trace and write.

u u u u u u u u

up   us   under   use

Write your own words.

Name

Copyright © Zaner-Bloser, Inc.   PRACTICE MASTER 43

PRACTICE MASTER 44

Trace and write.

U U U U U U U

Uma hummed a tune.

Write a name that begins with U.

Name

Copyright © Zaner-Bloser, Inc.   PRACTICE MASTER 44

Touch below the midline; curve back (left); curve forward (right), ending above the baseline.

Touch below the headline; curve back (left); curve forward (right), ending above the baseline.

MODEL

Write **s** on guidelines as you say the stroke descriptions. Give each child half a pipe cleaner to form into an **s**. Have children say the descriptions with you as they trace the **s**. Follow the same procedure for **S** using a whole pipe cleaner.

PRACTICE

Let children practice writing **s** and **S** on laminated writing cards or slates before they write on the pages.

Trace and write s.

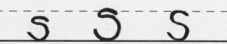

Trace and write S.

Trace and write words with s.

silly   songs

Trace and write names that begin with S.

Sari   Sid

Circle your best s and S.

Write your name.
Is there an s or S in your name?   Yes   No

58

EVALUATE

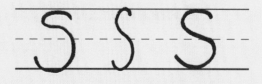

To help children evaluate their writing, ask questions such as these:
Does your **s** begin below the midline?
Are the spaces in the top and bottom of your **s** similar?
Does your **s** end above the baseline?

Is your **S** made with curve strokes?
Are the spaces in the top and bottom of your **S** similar?
Is the width of your **S** about the same as the model?

BETTER LETTERS

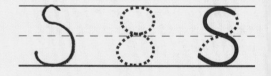

To help children write **s** with even curves, draw two circles, one above the other, between the midline and baseline. In color, outline the backward and forward curves of **s** that form part of a circle. Make other sets of circles and have children use them to write **s**.

To help children write the top and bottom of the **S** the same width, draw one circle above another circle as shown and outline the backward and forward curves of **S** that form part of a circle. Make other sets of circles and have children use them to write **S**.

Write each sentence.

I like most silly songs.

Sometimes I sing along.

On Your Own Write the kind of songs you like.

Circle your best word.

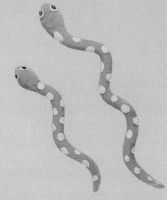

SILLY SNAKES

Provide clay for children to use. Have them roll the clay between their hands and then shape it into a long, long, long silly snake and then a short, short, short silly snake. Compare the sizes. Ask them to say /s/ as in *snake*. Have children repeat the activity, this time forming the letters s and **S**. Compare the sizes. Have children trace over the completed letters several times. (kinesthetic, visual)

WRITE SENTENCES

Before children write the two sentences on the page, call attention to the size and shape of letters. Ask them to find two letters that have the same shape but a different size. Ask which other lowercase and uppercase letter pairs have the same shape but different size. Invite comments on the size and shape of other letters. After children write, have them compare the size and shape of their letters with the models. Guide children to recognize why one letter might be better than another.

COACHING HINT

To call attention to letter shape, have children form forward and backward circles in the air. Encourage a free and easy motion as they form their circles. Then name one of the following letters and have the children form the shapes in the air: **g, G, j, J, q, Q, u, U, s,** and **S.** (kinesthetic)

PRACTICE MASTER 45

Trace and write.

s s s s s s s s

stop she says sky so

Write your own words.

Name

Copyright © Zaner-Bloser, Inc.   PRACTICE MASTER 45

PRACTICE MASTER 46

Trace and write.

S S S S S S S

Sasha sipped a soda.

Write a name that begins with S.

Name

Copyright © Zaner-Bloser, Inc.   PRACTICE MASTER 46

SURPRISE!

Prepare a surprise box with a set of textured alphabet letters. You may wish to use only the letters introduced so far. Have a volunteer, with eyes closed, pull a letter from the box, trace it with a finger, and try to name the letter. Continue until all the letters have been named. (kinesthetic)

Touch the headline; pull down straight to the baseline. Push up; circle forward (right) all the way around.

Touch the headline; pull down straight to the baseline. Lift. Touch the headline; slide right; curve forward (right) to the midline; slide left. Slide right; curve forward (right) to the baseline; slide left.

MODEL

Write **b** on guidelines as you say stroke descriptions. Have children trace the model **b** in their books as you repeat the descriptions. Follow the same procedure for **B**.

PRACTICE

Let children practice writing **b** and **B** on laminated writing cards or slates before they write on the pages.

Trace and write b.

Trace and write B.

Trace and write words with b.

but   better

Trace and write names that begin with B.

Bob   Beth

Write your name.
Is there a b or B in your name?   Yes   No

Circle your best b and B.

60

EVALUATE

To help children evaluate their writing, ask questions such as these:
Does your **b** begin at the headline?
Is your forward circle round?
Is your **b** straight up and down?

Does your **B** have two slide left strokes, one at the midline and one at the baseline?
Are the curves of your **B** round?
Is your **B** about the same width as the model?

BETTER LETTERS

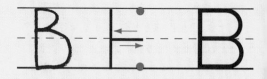

To help children begin **b** correctly, emphasize the importance of beginning with the correct stroke. Demonstrate the pull down straight stroke, the push up stroke and the forward circle, showing where to begin and end it.

To help the children write **B** with correct proportion, call attention to the retracing at the midline. Also remind children to make their slide right and slide left strokes the same width.

60

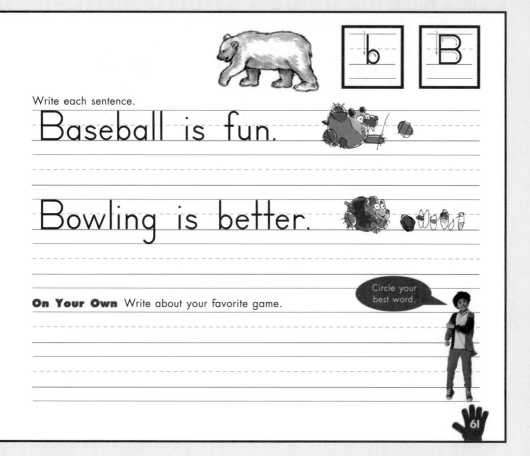

Write each sentence.

Baseball is fun.

Bowling is better.

On Your Own Write about your favorite game.

Circle your best word.

61

PHONICS CONNECTION

Ask children to listen as you say the words *brown bear*. Help them note that both *brown* and *bear* begin with the same sound—/b/. Read each set of words that follows: *black bear; red bear; baby bear; mother bear; big bear; friendly bear; best bear; beautiful bear*. After each, ask if the words begin alike. If the words begin alike, with /b/, ask one child to write **b** on guidelines on the chalkboard. (auditory, visual)

LETTER BINGO

Show children how to make a board for this letter game by folding writing paper into sixteen boxes. Invite children to write one uppercase or one lowercase letter in each box. Make a set of letter cards for the caller. To play, choose a letter card from the stack, call the letter, and have the children cover the letter with a marker if it appears on their game board. The first child to cover letters in a vertical, horizontal, or diagonal row is the winner. (visual, auditory)

WRITE SENTENCES

Before children write on the page, write the first sentence on the chalkboard, omitting spaces between words. Read the sentence and ask if it is written correctly. Elicit that the spaces between words are missing. Have children correct the sentence. After children write, have them compare their word spacing with the models. Guide children to recognize why one sentence might be better than another.

COACHING HINT

To help avoid confusion about when to use a backward circle or a forward circle, explain that if a circle in a letter comes before the vertical stroke, it is always a backward circle, as in **a**, **d**, **g**, and **q**. If a vertical stroke in a letter comes before the circle, the circle is always a forward circle, as in **b**. (visual)

PRACTICE MASTER 47

Trace and write.

b b b b b b b

boy   blue   bed   bird   be

Write your own words.

Name

Copyright © Zaner-Bloser, Inc.   PRACTICE MASTER 47

PRACTICE MASTER 48

Trace and write.

B B B B B B B

Bette buys books.

Write a name that begins with B.

Name

Copyright © Zaner-Bloser, Inc.   PRACTICE MASTER 48

Touch the midline; pull down straight through the baseline to the next guideline. Push up; circle forward (right) all the way around.

Touch the headline; pull down straight to the baseline. Lift. Touch the headline; slide right; curve forward (right) to the midline; slide left.

MODEL

Write **p** on guidelines as you say stroke descriptions. Model writing **p** in the air as you repeat the descriptions. Have children echo them as they write **p** in the air with you. Follow the same procedure for **P**.

PRACTICE

Let children practice writing **p** and **P** on laminated writing cards or slates before they write on the pages.

62

Trace and write p.

Trace and write P.

Trace and write words with p.

pilot   plane

Trace and write names that begin with P.

Pablo   Pat

Circle your best p and P.

Write your name.
Is there a p or P in your name?   Yes   No

62

EVALUATE

To help children evaluate their writing, ask questions such as these:
Does your **p** begin at the midline?
Is your forward circle round?
Does your **p** touch the headline of the next writing space?
Is your **p** straight up and down?

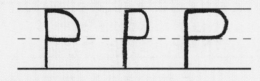

Is your **P** straight up and down?
Are your slide right and slide left strokes the same width?
Is your **P** about the same width as the model?

BETTER LETTERS

To help children make a round forward circle, make a pull down straight stroke that touches the next guideline; then place a dot halfway between the midline and baseline. Say stroke descriptions as children trace and write **p**.

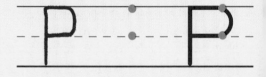

To help children write **P** the correct width, say the stroke descriptions, emphasizing the slide right and left strokes. Place dots to indicate where the slide right ends and where the slide left begins. Show how the curve is made between the two dots.

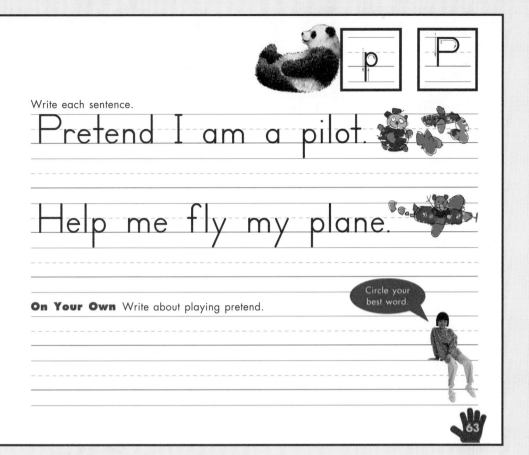

Write each sentence.

Pretend I am a pilot.

Help me fly my plane.

On Your Own Write about playing pretend.

Circle your best word.

63

PHONICS CONNECTION

Make available finger paint and paper. After children spread the paint, allow time for them to enjoy experimenting with writing letters. Ask what letter begins the word *panda*. After children agree that *panda* begins with **p**, ask them to write **p** if they hear a word that begins like *panda*. Say words that do and do not begin like *panda*. Repeat with names of people for **P**. (kinesthetic, auditory)

RHYME AND WRITE

Use the overhead projector to project **p** and **P** on the chalkboard. Say groups of rhyming words aloud, for example, *pat, sat, fat, cat; Jenny, Benny, Penny, Kenny; nest, pest, best, rest; dark, park, bark, lark.* Tell children to listen for the beginning sound and decide which word begins with /p/. Have a volunteer name the word and trace the projected **p** or **P** with a wet finger. Remind children to trace the uppercase letter if the word names a person. (auditory, kinesthetic)

WRITE SENTENCES

Before children write the two sentences on the page, call attention to the stroke formation of a particular letter. Ask where the letter begins and with which stroke. Remind children that it is important to begin a letter correctly. After they write, have them evaluate their letter formation by comparing their letters with the models. Guide children to recognize why one sentence might be better than another.

COACHING HINT

Review with children the use of the guidelines for correct letter formation. As you demonstrate on the chalkboard, have them draw over the baseline with a red crayon, over the headline with a blue crayon, and over the midline with a green crayon. (visual, kinesthetic)

PRACTICE MASTER 49

Trace and write.

p p p p p p p p

play pig people pie

Write your own words.

Name

Copyright © Zaner-Bloser, Inc.   PRACTICE MASTER 49

PRACTICE MASTER 50

Trace and write.

P P P P P P P P

Peter plays the piano.

Write a name that begins with P.

Name

Copyright © Zaner-Bloser, Inc.   PRACTICE MASTER 50

On guidelines on the chalkboard write **uU**, **sS**, **bB**, and **pP**. Have children take turns naming the letter pairs and pointing to each uppercase and lowercase letter.

Call attention to the size and shape of letters by asking questions such as these: Which letters are tall? Which letters begin with a pull down straight stroke? Which short letter goes below the baseline? Which letters look alike except for their size?

MODEL

Write **uU** on guidelines as you say the stroke descriptions for each letter. Model writing the letters in the air as you repeat the descriptions. Have children echo them as they write letters in the air with you. Follow the same procedure for **sS**, **bB**, and **pP**.

PRACTICE

Let children practice writing the letter pairs **uU**, **sS**, **bB**, and **pP** on laminated writing cards or slates before they write on the pages.

Review Write the letters.

uU   sS   bB   pP

Use the letters to write words.

pup   bug   use   bib

Write your name.

Circle your best word.

64

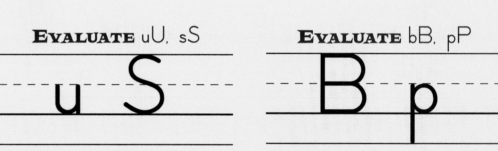

EVALUATE uU, sS

u S

To help children evaluate their writing, ask questions such as these:
Does your **u** begin at the midline?
Are the pull down straight and push up strokes in your **U** straight?
Are the top and bottom of your **s** similar?
Does your **S** begin below the headline?

EVALUATE bB, pP

B p

To help children evaluate their writing, ask questions such as these:
Is the forward circle in your **b** round?
Are the curves in your **B** the same size?
Is the forward circle in your **p** round?
Does your **P** begin with a pull down straight stroke?

Write the sentences.

Stand straight.

Put your hands up.

Bend and stretch.

Put a 😊 next to your best sentence.

My Words

IDEAS FOR EXERCISE

Ask children to develop a list of games and exercises they enjoy. Distribute writing paper and have them write their first two choices from the list. (visual, kinesthetic)

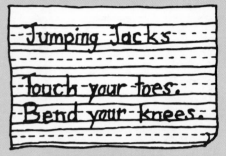

HANDS CAN

Share ideas about the different things we do with our hands. Write a list of action words on the chalkboard. Use the ideas to write a poem with a simple rhyme pattern.

Hands can clap,
They can snap.
Hands can write,
And hold you tight.

(auditory, kinesthetic)

WRITE SENTENCES

Before children write on the page, write a sentence on the chalkboard without spaces between words. Ask if the sentence is hard to read. Help children recognize the reason for correct spacing. Choose a volunteer to indicate where the spaces should be and to rewrite the sentence correctly. After they write, have children compare their word spacing with the models. Guide them to recognize why one sentence might be better than another.

COACHING HINT

Children having difficulty with motor skills may benefit from the increased writing space the chalkboard provides. To help them practice writing sentences, print a three-word sentence on a sentence strip. Cut it apart and ask one child to arrange the words into a sentence and to write it on the board. Have classmates check the spacing between words. (visual)

MY WORDS

Ask children to write words of their own. Encourage them to write words that contain the review letters. If they need help, suggest they look for words on the previous pages.

Touch the midline; pull down straight to the baseline. Push up; curve forward (right).

Touch the headline; pull down straight to the baseline. Lift. Touch the headline; slide right; curve forward (right) to the midline; slide left. Slant right to the baseline.

MODEL

Write **r** on guidelines as you say the stroke descriptions. Have children use their fingers to write **r** on their desks as you repeat the descriptions and children echo them. Follow the same procedure for **R**.

PRACTICE

Let children practice writing **r** and **R** on laminated writing cards or slates before they write on the pages.

Trace and write r.

Trace and write R.

Trace and write words with r.

run   roll

Trace and write names that begin with R.

Reba   Ron

Write your name.
Is there an r or R in your name?   Yes   No

Circle your best r and R.

66

EVALUATE

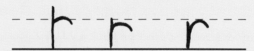

To help children evaluate their writing, ask questions such as these:
Does your **r** begin at the midline?
Does your curve forward stroke end below the midline?

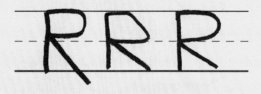

Does your slant right stroke begin at the midline and touch the baseline?
Are your slide right and slide left strokes the same width?
Is your **R** about the same width as the model?

BETTER LETTERS

To help children avoid writing **r** with a loop, have them carefully retrace the pull down straight stroke. To show where to start and finish the curve forward stroke of **r**, add dots and have children complete the letter.

To help children write a slant right stroke, demonstrate how to make the stroke from the midline to baseline. Write **R** omitting the slant right stroke. As you say descriptions, have them trace and complete **R**.

Write each sentence.

Running is easy for me.

Roller blading is hard.

On Your Own Write about something that is easy for you to do.

Circle your best word.

67

LETTER RIDDLES

Try this letter riddle with your class. List the following letters on the chalkboard: **r, p, b, s, u,** and **q.** Then say:

I am a letter with a descender.
I have a circle forward stroke.
I come after o in the alphabet.
Which letter am I?

Ask more riddles and invite children to make up some riddles of their own. (visual, auditory)

WRITE SENTENCES

Before children write the two sentences on the page, emphasize that manuscript writing is straight up and down. Write the second sentence on the chalkboard. Using colored chalk, lightly draw parallel vertical lines over the vertical strokes to show good vertical quality. After children write, have them decide if their letters are straight up and down like the models. Guide children to recognize why one word might be better than another.

PRACTICE MASTER 51

Trace and write.

r r r r r r r r

read run rock rain

Write your own words.

Name

Copyright © Zaner-Bloser, Inc.   PRACTICE MASTER 51

CATEGORY FUN

List these four categories on the chalkboard: Girls' Names, Boys' Names, Food, and Animals. Invite children to brainstorm words that begin with **r** or **R** for each category. Write their responses and ask volunteers to trace over the letters **r** and **R** with colored chalk. Add other categories to extend the game. (auditory)

COACHING HINT

You can evaluate the vertical quality of children's handwriting by drawing pencil lines through the vertical strokes of their letters. If the lines are parallel, the vertical quality is correct.

PRACTICE MASTER 52

Trace and write.

R R R R R R R

Ruth ran the race.

Write a name that begins with R.

Name

Copyright © Zaner-Bloser, Inc.   PRACTICE MASTER 52

ALPHABET BIG BOOK

Update the Alphabet Big Book by adding pages with labeled drawings for each new letter.

Touch the midline; pull down straight to the baseline. Push up; curve forward (right); pull down straight to the baseline.

Touch the headline; pull down straight to the baseline. Lift. Touch the headline; slant right to the baseline. Push up straight to the headline.

MODEL

Write **n** on guidelines as you say the stroke descriptions. Model writing **n** on sandpaper. Pair children and have them take turns writing and saying descriptions. Follow the same procedure for **N**.

PRACTICE

Let children practice writing **n** and **N** on laminated writing cards or slates before they write on the pages.

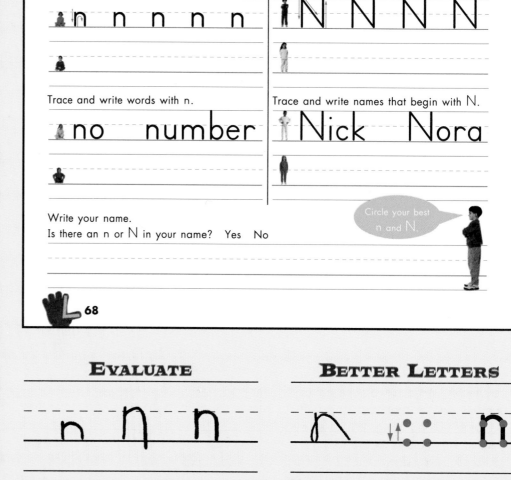

Trace and write n.

n n n n

Trace and write N.

N N N N

Trace and write words with n.

no number

Trace and write names that begin with N.

Nick Nora

Write your name.
Is there an n or N in your name?   Yes   No

Circle your best n and N.

68

EVALUATE

To help children evaluate their writing, ask questions such as these:
Does your **n** touch the midline?
Does your **n** end at the baseline?
Are your pull down strokes straight?
Is your **n** straight up and down?

Does your **N** begin at the headline?
Are your strokes straight?
Does your push up straight stroke end at the headline?
Is your **N** about the same width as the model?

BETTER LETTERS

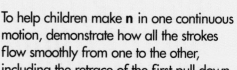

To help children make **n** in one continuous motion, demonstrate how all the strokes flow smoothly from one to the other, including the retrace of the first pull down straight stroke. Remind them not to lift their pencils.

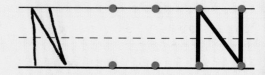

To help children write **N** the correct width, place dots as shown and ask them to write the letter as you say the stroke descriptions. Call attention to the width of the slant line and suggest children try to make their slant lines the same width.

Write each sentence.

Now I know numbers.

I can count past twenty.

On Your Own Write about something you can do with numbers.

Circle your best word.

NOODLE-BETS

Collect different-shaped pastas. Display them and have children describe the shapes. Point out shapes that are straight up and down or that have circles. Invite children to use the shapes to form alphabet or "noodle-bet" letters. Ask them to keep a list of the letters they make. (visual, kinesthetic)

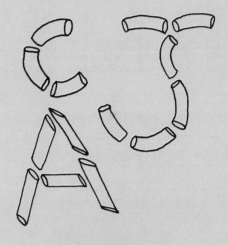

WRITE SENTENCES

Before children write the sentences on the page, emphasize that manuscript writing is straight up and down. Write *numbers* correctly on the chalkboard and then write it again with the letters slanting left or right. Discuss which model is correct and why. After children write, have them compare their letters with the model to see if they are straight up and down. Guide children to recognize why one word might be better than another.

PRACTICE MASTER 53

Trace and write.

n n n n n n n

not   name   night   need

Write your own words.

Name

Copyright © Zaner-Bloser, Inc.   PRACTICE MASTER 53

COACHING HINT

Demonstrate for children the technique of drawing a horizontal line with a ruler along the tops of their letters to show proper size. Have them practice this technique periodically. (visual)

PRACTICE MASTER 54

Trace and write.

N N N N N N N

Nate naps until noon.

Write a name that begins with N.

Name

Copyright © Zaner-Bloser, Inc.   PRACTICE MASTER 54

PHONICS CONNECTION

Write the word *noon* in large letters across the chalkboard. Point out that *noon* begins and ends with **n**. Print the following words on cards: *nice, nose, fan, pin, hen, night.* Ask children to listen for the beginning and ending sounds as you read each word. If the word begins like *noon,* have a child tape the word under the initial **n**. If it ends like *noon,* have a child tape the word under the final **n**. (visual, auditory)

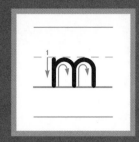

Touch the midline; pull down straight to the baseline. Push up; curve forward (right); pull down straight to the baseline. Push up; curve forward (right); pull down straight to the baseline.

Touch the headline; pull down straight to the baseline. Lift. Touch the headline; slant right to the baseline. Slant up (right) to the headline. Pull down straight to the baseline.

MODEL

Write **m** on guidelines as you say the stroke descriptions. In turn, ask children to dip their fingers into water and to write **m** on the chalkboard as they say the descriptions together. Follow the same procedure for **M**.

PRACTICE

Let children practice writing **m** and **M** on laminated writing cards or slates before they write on the pages.

70

Trace and write m.

m m m m

Trace and write M.

M M M

Trace and write words with m.

moon may

Trace and write names that begin with M.

Min Matt

Write your name.
Is there an m or M in your name?   Yes   No

Circle your best m and M.

70

EVALUATE

To help children evaluate their writing, ask questions such as these:
Does your **m** begin at the midline?
Does your **m** have three pull down straight strokes?
Are the tops of the curve strokes round?

Does your **M** rest on the baseline?
Is your **M** about the same width as the model?

BETTER LETTERS

To help children make **m** the correct width, place three dots as shown. Use the dots to demonstrate how to write **m** in one continuous motion. Point out the two look-alike parts in **m** by tracing them in different colors.

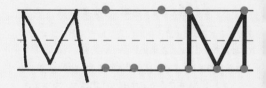

To help children make **M** the correct width, place dots as shown. Say the strokes and have children connect the dots, lifting the pencil only once, after the first stroke.

Write each sentence.

Look at the moon.

Maybe I will go there.

On Your Own Write about a place you might go.

Circle your best word.

71

WRITE SENTENCES

Before children write the two sentences on the page, have them compare the formation of the letters **m** and **n** in the word *moon*. Note similarities in size and shape. After children write, have them compare their letters with the models. Guide children to recognize why one word might be better than another.

COACHING HINT

Holding the pencil too tightly is a common problem that causes children to tire easily when writing. To overcome this problem, have children crumple a piece of paper, place it in the palms of their writing hand, and pick up the pencil. This will serve as a reminder not to squeeze the pencil. (kinesthetic)

PRACTICE MASTER 55

Trace and write.

m   m   m   m   m   m   m

me   mother   man   more

Write your own words.

Name

Copyright © Zaner-Bloser, Inc.   PRACTICE MASTER 55

PRACTICE MASTER 56

Trace and write.

M   M   M   M   M   M

Martha makes me smile.

Write a name that begins with M.

Name

Copyright © Zaner-Bloser, Inc.   PRACTICE MASTER 56

WRITING CORNER

Invite children to help you write silly sentences about monkeys. Use several words that begin with the same sound. Pair children and let them work together. Here are some examples to help you get started. *Monkeys munch on marvelous muffins. Monkeys march merrily in May.* Extend the activity to writing about other animals using different letters. (auditory, visual)

MONKEY SEE AND DO

Choose a volunteer to be the "monkey" of the moment. Ask the child to write **m** or **M** on guidelines on the chalkboard. Then ask the "monkey" to choose another child to "see and do" the same. As the game continues, select different children to take the roles and encourage the "monkey" to write words or sentences as well. (visual)

71

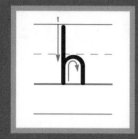

Touch the headline; pull down straight to the base-line. Push up; curve forward (right); pull down straight to the baseline.

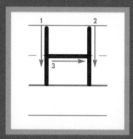

Touch the headline; pull down straight to the base-line. Lift. Move to the right and touch the headline; pull down straight to the base-line. Lift. Move to the left and touch the midline; slide right.

MODEL

Write **h** on guidelines as you say the stroke descrip-tions. Have children trace the model **h** in their books as you repeat the stroke descriptions. Then have them say the stroke descrip-tions with you as they trace **h** again. Follow the same procedure for **H**.

PRACTICE

Let children practice writing **h** and **H** on laminated writ-ing cards or slates before they write on the pages.

72

Trace and write h.

Trace and write H.

Trace and write words with h.

hit   home

Trace and write names that begin with H.

Hal Hope

Circle your best
h and H.

Write your name.
Is there an h or H in your name?   Yes   No

72

EVALUATE

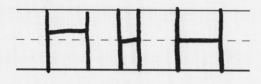

To help children evaluate their writing, ask questions such as these:
Are your pull down straight strokes straight?
Does your **h** touch the headline and baseline?

Is your slide right stroke on the midline?
Is your **H** straight up and down?
Is your **H** about the same width as the model?

BETTER LETTERS

To help children begin and end the for-ward curve of **h** correctly, write **h** and put a dot at the start and end of the curve. Point out that the curve touches the midline. Remind children to make straight vertical lines on both sides of the curve forward stroke.

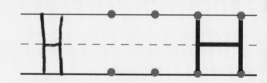

To help children write **H** the correct width, show them how to use their index fingers to measure the space between the two pull down straight strokes. Have them practice this spacing as they write. If the letter slants, check paper positioning.

Write each sentence.

I hit a home run.

Hurrah for me!

On Your Own Write about something that makes you proud.

Circle your best word.

73

PHONICS CONNECTION

Introduce this game by describing a hungry hippo you know who will eat anything, so long as what he eats begins with the same sound that begins *hippo*. Start the game and soon the children will be able to join. *I know a hippo who loves to eat. He eats hens, but he never eats chickens. He eats hats, but he never eats socks.* (auditory)

LETTER HUNT

Hide letter cards around the classroom. Then ask children to go on a letter hunt. Encourage them to sing "A-Hunting We Will Go" as they search for the letters. After a few minutes, let them show each letter they found, write the letter on guidelines on the chalkboard, and name a word that begins with the same letter. (visual, auditory)

WRITE SENTENCES

Before children write the two sentences on the page, write *Hurrah* on the chalkboard. Have them compare the size and shape of the letters **H** and **h**. Ask them to name other tall letters in the sentences on the page. After they write on the page, have them compare the size and the shape of their letters with the models. Guide children to recognize why one word might be better than another.

COACHING HINT

Any tendency to twist the hand or wrist by the left-handed child should be corrected early. The twisting and turning is often an attempt to see the paper, so correct paper position is vital.

PRACTICE MASTER 57

Trace and write.

h h h h h h h h

help   hide   happy   here

Write your own words.

Name

Copyright © Zaner-Bloser, Inc.   PRACTICE MASTER 57

PRACTICE MASTER 58

Trace and write.

H H H H H H

Hank helps at home.

Write a name that begins with H.

Name

Copyright © Zaner-Bloser, Inc.   PRACTICE MASTER 58

BEFORE WRITING

On guidelines on the chalkboard write **rR, nN, mM,** and **hH.** Have children take turns naming the letter pairs and pointing to each uppercase and lowercase letter.

Call attention to the size and shape of letters by asking questions such as these:
Which letters are short?
Which stroke begins all these letters?
Which letters have retraces?
Which letters have slant strokes?

MODEL

Write **rR** on guidelines as you say the stroke descriptions for each letter. Model writing the letters in the air as you repeat the descriptions. Have children echo them as they write the letters in the air with you. Follow the same procedure for **nN, mM,** and **hH.**

PRACTICE

Let children practice writing the letter pairs **rR, nN, mM,** and **hH** on laminated writing cards or slates before they write on the pages.

74

Review   Write the letters.

rR   nN   mM   hH

Use the letters to write words.

rain   name   mine   hear

Write your name.

Circle your best word.

74

EVALUATE rR, nN

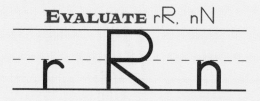

r R n

To help children evaluate their writing, ask questions such as these:
Does the curve forward in your **r** end below the midline?
Is your **R** about the same width as the model?
Are the pull down straight strokes in your **n** straight?
Does your **N** rest on the baseline?

EVALUATE mM, hH

M h

To help children evaluate their writing, ask questions such as these:
Does your **m** have three pull down straight strokes?
Is your **M** about the same width as the model?
Does your **h** touch the headline and baseline?
Are all the strokes in your **H** straight?

Write the sentences.

Happy birthday!

Make a wish first.

Now we can cut the cake.

Put a ☺ next to your best sentence.

My Words

WRITE SENTENCES

Before children write the sentences on the page, point out that manuscript letters should be straight up and down. Write one of the sentences on guidelines on the chalkboard. Make several letters slant left or right. Have children take turns circling letters that are not vertical. After they write, tell them to compare the slant of their letters with the models. Guide children to recognize why one sentence might be better than another.

MY WORDS

Ask children to write words of their own. Encourage them to write words that contain the review letters. If they need help, suggest they look for words on the previous pages.

COACHING HINT

A right-handed child when writing at the chalkboard should stand in front of his or her writing and pull the downstrokes toward his or her midsection. The elbow is slightly bent, and the writing is done at a comfortable height on the chalkboard (between eyes and chin). As the writing progresses across the board, have the child move to the right to keep the downstrokes vertical. (kinesthetic)

A BIRTHDAY SURPRISE

Invite children to help plan a surprise birthday party for a familiar storybook character. After they choose a character, help them develop two lists. The first list should include the names of other characters to invite to the party. The second list should include items needed for the party. Have children share their lists and draw pictures to show the imaginary celebration. (visual)

WISH LISTS

Since wishing is sometimes a part of birthday celebrations, ask children to think about wishes and to write wish lists of things they might wish to do or see on their next birthday. Talk about things they might include. After the lists are completed, ask volunteers to share their lists. (visual)

Touch the midline; slant right to the baseline. Slant up (right) to the midline.

Touch the headline; slant right to the baseline. Slant up (right) to the headline.

MODEL

Write **v** and **V** on guidelines as you say the stroke descriptions. Have children compare the size and formation of the letters. Show them how to form a **v** by holding two fingers on a slant and tracing **v** as they say the descriptions with you.

PRACTICE

Let children practice writing **v** and **V** on laminated writing cards or slates before they write on the pages.

76

Trace and write v.

Trace and write V.

Trace and write words with v.

very love

Trace and write names that begin with V.

Violet Van

Write your name.
Is there a v or V in your name?   Yes   No

Circle your best v and V.

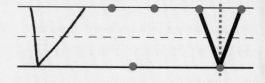

76

EVALUATE

To help children evaluate their writing, ask questions such as these:
Are your slant strokes straight?
Does your **v** touch both the midline and baseline?

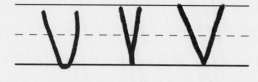

Are your slant strokes straight?
Is your **V** about the same width as the model?

BETTER LETTERS

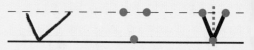

To help children write **v** the correct width, place two dots on the midline and one between them on the baseline. Have children connect the dots with the slant strokes as you say the descriptions. Draw a dotted vertical line down the center to show that the two sides of **v** are the same width.

To help children write **V** the correct width, follow the same procedure as with **v** but put the two dots on the headline and a third dot between them on the baseline.

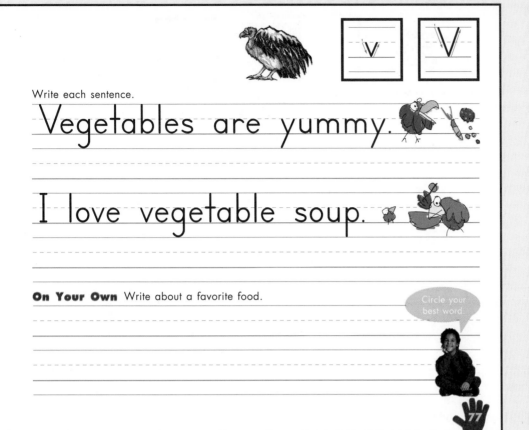

Write each sentence.

Vegetables are yummy.

I love vegetable soup.

On Your Own Write about a favorite food.

Circle your best word.

77

PRACTICE MASTER 59

Trace and write.

V V V V V V V V

very   vest   vine   van

Write your own words.

Name

Copyright © Zaner-Bloser, Inc.   PRACTICE MASTER 59

PRACTICE MASTER 60

Trace and write.

V V V V V V

Vera visited Virginia.

Write a name that begins with V.

Name

Copyright © Zaner-Bloser, Inc.   PRACTICE MASTER 60

77

Touch the midline; slant right to the baseline. Lift. Move to the right and touch the midline; slant left through the baseline.

Touch the headline; slant right to the midline. Lift. Move to the right and touch the headline; slant left to the midline. Pull down straight to the baseline.

MODEL

Write **y** on guidelines as you say the stroke descriptions. Model writing **y** in the air as you say the descriptions. Have children echo them as they write **y** in the air with you. Follow the same procedure for **Y**.

PRACTICE

Let children practice writing **y** and **Y** on laminated writing cards or slates before they write on the pages.

78

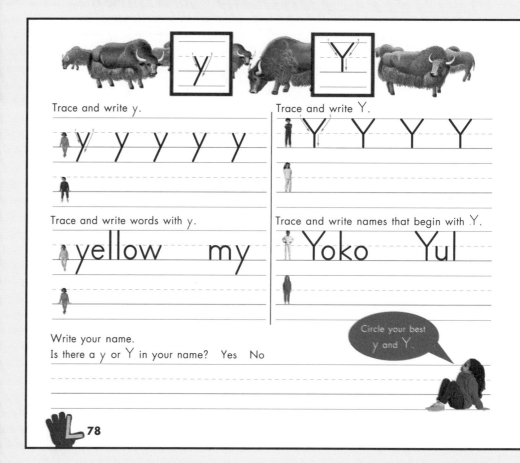

Trace and write y.

Trace and write Y.

Trace and write words with y.

yellow   my

Trace and write names that begin with Y.

Yoko   Yul

Circle your best y and Y.

Write your name.
Is there a y or Y in your name?   Yes   No

78

EVALUATE

To help children evaluate their writing, ask questions such as these:
Are your slant strokes straight?
Does your slant right stroke stop at the baseline?
Does your **y** touch the headline of the next writing space?

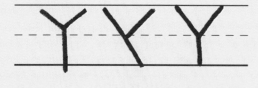

Do your slant strokes meet at the midline?
Are your strokes straight?
Does your **Y** end with a pull down straight stroke?

BETTER LETTERS

To help children write the second stroke of **y** correctly, write models of the letter **y** with the second stroke shown as a dotted line for children to trace.

To help children see that **Y** is formed with two slant strokes and one pull down straight stroke, write three models of **Y**, each with a different stroke dotted. Have children write or trace the **Y** as you say the stroke descriptions. Demonstrate how to stop after the second slant stroke before pulling down straight.

Write each sentence.

Yellow is a pretty color.

Red is my favorite.

On Your Own Write about your favorite color.

Circle your best word.

79

FuN and GameS

LETTERS BY THE YARD

Group the children and have them watch as you measure a yard of paper from a roll. Ask them to work cooperatively to fill the yard of paper with a yard of writing. Let them decide whether to write letters, words, or sentences and how to divide the task. Remind them to use correct spacing. Display their completed work. (visual)

YES/NO GAME

Prepare two index cards with guidelines for each child. Have children write *yes* on one card and *no* on the other. Use the cards to play a listening game. State a fact or an opinion similar to those that follow. Ask children to hold up a card to indicate their answer.

L comes after M in the alphabet.
I like to read.
Yaks are large animals.

(visual, auditory)

WRITE SENTENCES

Before children write the sentences on the page, write on guidelines: *What is your favorite color? Is it yellow?* Ask children how many sentences you have written and how they know. Point out that the space between sentences is larger than the space between words. After they write, have them compare their spacing with that in the models. Guide children to recognize why one sentence might be better than another.

PRACTICE MASTER 61

Trace and write.

Y y y y y y y y

you   yell   yes   yard

Write your own words.

Name

Copyright © Zaner-Bloser, Inc.   PRACTICE MASTER 61

COACHING HINT

Use a form of reciprocal teaching to reinforce correct formation of letters. Have children take turns demonstrating letter formation. Remind them to use correct terms and stroke descriptions and to refer to guidelines. Teacher direction is important, but children should be encouraged to take the lead as much as possible. (visual, auditory)

PRACTICE MASTER 62

Trace and write.

Y Y Y Y Y Y Y

Yoshie plays every day.

Write a name that begins with Y.

Name

Copyright © Zaner-Bloser, Inc.   PRACTICE MASTER 62

79

Touch the midline; slant right to the baseline. Slant up (right) to the midline. Slant right to the baseline. Slant up (right) to the midline.

Touch the headline; slant right to the baseline. Slant up (right) to the headline. Slant right to the baseline. Slant up (right) to the headline.

MODEL

Write **w** on guidelines as you say the stroke descriptions. Have children trace the model **w** in their books as you repeat the descriptions. Follow the same procedure for **W**.

PRACTICE

Let children practice writing **w** and **W** on laminated writing cards or slates before they write on the pages.

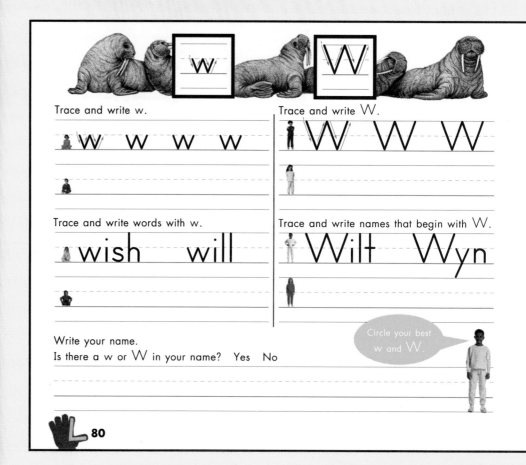

Trace and write w.

Trace and write W.

Trace and write words with w.

wish   will

Trace and write names that begin with W.

Wilt   Wyn

Write your name.
Is there a w or W in your name?   Yes   No

Circle your best w and W.

EVALUATE

To help children evaluate their writing, ask questions such as these:
Does your **w** have four straight slant strokes?
Is your **w** about the same width as the model?

Are the four slant strokes of your **W** straight?
Is your **W** about the same width as the model?

BETTER LETTERS

To help children write **w** with straight slant strokes, say the stroke descriptions as they write. Remind them not to lift their pencils when they make the slant strokes. Place dots as shown to help them make their slant strokes an even width.

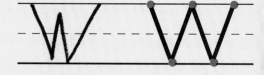

To help children write **W** the correct width, place dots on the headline and baseline as shown. Point out that **W** and **w** differ in size but not in stroke formation. Stress the importance of using the guidelines.

Write each sentence.

I wish I could whistle.

Wow! What fun!

On Your Own Write about something you wish you could do.

Circle your best word.

81

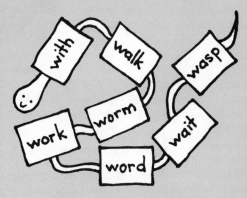
WORD WORM

Distribute index cards with guidelines. After everyone agrees that *worm* begins with **w**, ask children to write a word that begins with **w** on each card. Encourage the use of dictionaries and other books for ideas. Arrange the cards to form a word worm. See how far your word worm will travel. Have volunteers add a face and other details. (visual)

ACTION WORD CHARADES

Choose one player to act out an action word for classmates to guess. Remind children they are not allowed to give any oral clues, but explain that they can give one written clue by writing on the chalkboard the letter that begins the action word. Then let the acting and guessing begin. (visual)

WRITE SENTENCES

Before children write the three sentences on this page, call attention to the spacing between words. Have children place a finger between words as a reminder to leave that much space. Help them compare their word spacing with that in the models. Guide children to recognize why one sentence might be better than another.

COACHING HINT

Using card stock or other heavy paper, cut out the parts of a letter (basic strokes) and have children put the parts together to form the letter. (visual, kinesthetic)

PRACTICE MASTER 63

Trace and write.

W W W W W W W

we want word well

Write your own words.

Name

Copyright © Zaner-Bloser, Inc.   PRACTICE MASTER 63

PRACTICE MASTER 64

Trace and write.

W W W W W

Wayne always wins.

Write a name that begins with W.

Name

Copyright © Zaner-Bloser, Inc.   PRACTICE MASTER 64

Touch the midline; slant right to the baseline. Lift. Move to the right and touch the midline; slant left to the baseline.

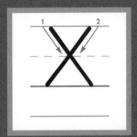

Touch the headline; slant right to the baseline. Lift. Move to the right and touch the headline; slant left to the baseline.

MODEL

Write **x** and **X** on guidelines as you say the stroke descriptions. Have children compare the size and formation of the letters. Ask them to write **x** and **X** on their desks with their fingers as you say the descriptions together.

PRACTICE

Let children practice writing **x** and **X** on laminated writing cards or slates before they write on the pages.

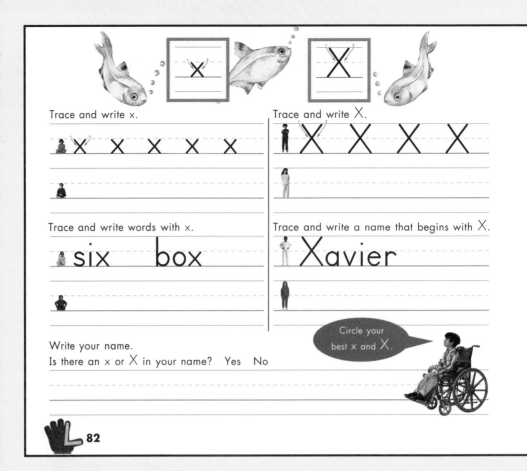

Trace and write x.

Trace and write X.

Trace and write words with x.

six box

Trace and write a name that begins with X.

Xavier

Write your name.
Is there an x or X in your name?   Yes   No

Circle your best x and X.

EVALUATE

To help children evaluate their writing, ask questions such as these:
Are your slant strokes straight?
Does your **x** touch the midline and baseline?
Do your slant strokes cross halfway between the midline and the baseline?

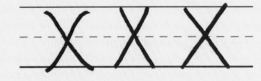

Are your slant strokes straight?
Do your slant strokes cross at the midline?
Is your **X** about the same width as the model?

BETTER LETTERS

To help children cross the slant strokes in **x** correctly, have them first make the slant right stroke. Place a dot on the midline where the slant left stroke should begin. Tell children to aim the second slant stroke at the halfway point on the first slant stroke.

To help children cross the slant lines in **X** correctly, remind them to aim the second stroke so that it crosses the first stroke at the midline. Place a dot on the headline where the slant left stroke should begin.

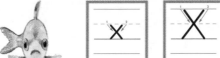

FUN and GAMES

Write each sentence.

I am an excellent writer.

X is my best letter.

On Your Own Write about your best uppercase letter.

Circle your best word.

83

WRITE SENTENCES

Before children write the two sentences, call attention to letters with slant strokes. Have children find and trace a letter that has two slant strokes that cross. After they write, have them compare the size and the shape of their slant letters with the models. Guide children to recognize why one word might be better than another.

COACHING HINT

The development and maintenance of good handwriting skills depend on meaningful practice. Too much practice of letters in isolation will discourage most children. Possible writing activities include friendly letters, jokes and riddles, nametags or labels, charts, vocabulary cards, and simple stories or poems. Writing may be done in cooperative groups.

PRACTICE MASTER 65

Trace and write.

x x x x x x x x

mix   ox   box   next   fix

Write your own words.

Name

Copyright © Zaner-Bloser, Inc.   PRACTICE MASTER 65

PRACTICE MASTER 66

Trace and write.

X X X X X X X

Xylon saw six foxes.

Write a name that begins with X.

Name

Copyright © Zaner-Bloser, Inc.   PRACTICE MASTER 66

WRITING CORNER

Point out that **x** is a letter that does not begin many words but can be found in other positions in words. Write words that have the letter **x**, such as *box*, *six*, *excellent*, and *Texas*. Choose volunteers to use their fingers to trace the **x** in each word. Provide dictionaries for children to use and have them work in pairs to search for words with **x**. Ask them to list words they find and share their completed lists. (visual)

NAME THAT LETTER

Name a category of letters. Start with letters that have slant lines. Invite children to work in small groups at the chalkboard to recall and write letters with slant lines. Repeat with other categories. (visual)

ALPHABET BIG BOOK

Update the class Alphabet Big Book by adding pages for each new letter.

83

CONTINUOUS STROKE

Touch the headline; pull down straight to the base-line. Lift. Move to the right and touch the midline; slant left. Slant right to the baseline.

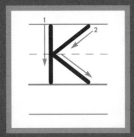

Touch the headline; pull down straight to the base-line. Lift. Move to the right and touch the headline; slant left to the midline. Slant right to the baseline.

MODEL

Write **k** on guidelines as you say the stroke descriptions. Invite children to trace the model **k** in their books as you repeat the descriptions. Follow the same procedure for **K**.

PRACTICE

Let children practice writing **k** and **K** on laminated writing cards or slates before they write on the pages.

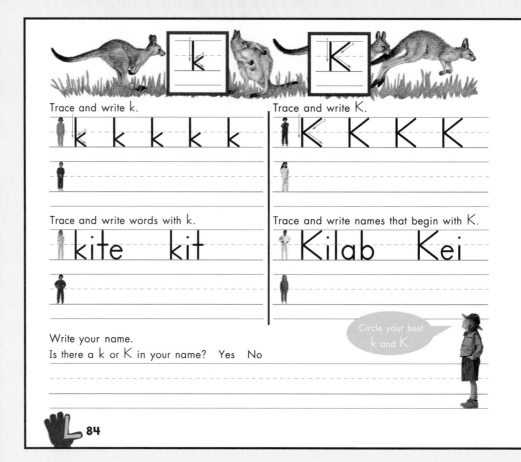

Trace and write k.

Trace and write K.

Trace and write words with k.

kite   kit

Trace and write names that begin with K.

Kilab   Kei

Write your name.
Is there a k or K in your name?   Yes   No

Circle your best k and K.

EVALUATE

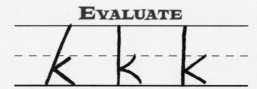

To help children evaluate their writing, ask questions such as these:
Is your **k** straight up and down?
Are your slant strokes straight?
Does your slant left stroke end at the pull down straight stroke?

Is your **K** straight up and down?
Does your slant left line begin at the head-line and end at the midline?
Do your two slant strokes meet at the midline?

BETTER LETTERS

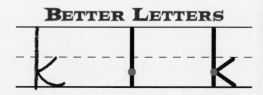

To help children correctly write the slant strokes in **k**, make a pull down straight stroke and place a dot on the line halfway between the midline and the baseline. Note this stopping point for the end of the first slant stroke. Have children complete **k** with two slant strokes that touch the dot.

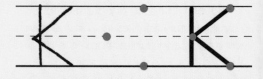

To help children correctly write the slant strokes in **K**, show how the slant left stroke stops on the midline where the slant right stroke begins. Place a dot on the headline and the baseline to show the width of **K**.

Write each sentence.

I made a kite.

Kites are easy to make.

On Your Own Write about something that is easy to make.

Circle your best word.

85

PHONICS CONNECTION

Play this game to music. Invite children to sit in a circle. Place a slate and chalk in the center. As the music plays, have children pass a **Kk** letter card around the circle. When the music stops, direct the child holding the card to write **K** or **k** on the slate in the center and say a word that begins with **k** such as *kangaroo*. After this round, continue the game with other letters. (auditory)

RHYME AND WRITE

Write a list of words on guidelines on the chalkboard, for example, *black, rock, look, seek, like,* and *take.* Read each word. Ask a volunteer to say a word that rhymes and write it on the chalkboard. Read aloud the rhyming pairs. Point out the letter **k** in each word. (auditory)

WRITE SENTENCES

Before children write the two sentences on the page, point out that all the letters are straight up and down. Review which letters are short or tall and which have descenders. After children write, have them evaluate the vertical quality and the size of their letters by comparing them with the models. Guide children to recognize why one sentence might be better than another.

COACHING HINT

Review uppercase letters with slant strokes. Write **M, N, W, V, X,** and **K** on the chalkboard. Have children choose two letters to compare. Ask: *How are they alike? How are they different? Which strokes are the same? Which letter has the most strokes?* Repeat with circle letters **O, C, Q,** and **G** or straight line letters **L, I, T, E, F,** and **H.** (visual)

PRACTICE MASTER 67

Trace and write.

k   k   k   k   k   k   k   k

king   kiss   kitten   kind

Write your own words.

Name

Copyright © Zaner-Bloser, Inc.   PRACTICE MASTER 67

PRACTICE MASTER 68

Trace and write.

K   K   K   K   K   K   K

Kimiko likes the kitten.

Write a name that begins with K.

Name

Copyright © Zaner-Bloser, Inc.   PRACTICE MASTER 68

Touch the midline; slide right. Slant left to the baseline. Slide right.

Touch the headline; slide right. Slant left to the baseline. Slide right.

MODEL

Write **z** on guidelines as you say stroke descriptions. Model writing **z** in the air as you repeat the descriptions. Have children echo them as they write **z** in the air with you. Follow the same procedure for **Z**.

PRACTICE

Let children practice writing **z** and **Z** on laminated writing cards or slates before they write on the pages.

Trace and write z.

Trace and write Z.

Trace and write words with z.

sneeze   zoo

Trace and write names that begin with Z.

Zina   Zach

Write your name.
Is there a z or Z in your name?   Yes   No

Circle your best z and Z.

86

EVALUATE

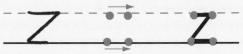

To help children evaluate their writing, ask questions such as these:
Is your **z** about the same width as the model?
Are the top and bottom strokes of your **z** the same width?

Is your **Z** about the same width as the model?
Are the top and bottom strokes of your **Z** the same width?
Are your lines straight?

BETTER LETTERS

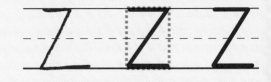

To help children write **z** with straight lines, demonstrate how to stop before and after the slant left stroke. Remind children not to lift their pencils and to make sure the two slide right lines are the same width.

To help children make the top and bottom strokes of **Z**, write **Z** and draw lines to enclose it in a box.

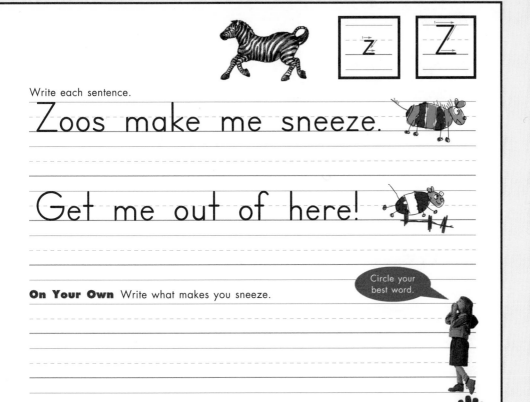

Write each sentence.

Zoos make me sneeze.

Get me out of here!

On Your Own Write what makes you sneeze.

Circle your best word.

87

SPAGHETTI LETTERS

Invite children to use dry spaghetti to form the straight line and slant letters they have been learning. Demonstrate how to break the spaghetti and how to match the size of the pieces. Have children glue each spaghetti letter to an index card and then write the letter below it. (visual, kinesthetic)

WRITE SENTENCES

Before children write the two sentences on the page, ask a volunteer to say the stroke descriptions for the two uppercase letters shown. After they write, have them compare their letters with the models. Invite them to summarize what they know about correct spacing of letters in words and of words in sentences. Guide children to recognize why one sentence might be better than another.

COACHING HINT

Continue to emphasize the importance of good handwriting in all subject areas. Provide writing activities that encourage children's immediate application of handwriting skills.

PRACTICE MASTER 69

Trace and write.

Z Z Z Z Z Z Z Z

zip zoom daze maze

Write your own words.

Name

Copyright © Zaner-Bloser, Inc.   PRACTICE MASTER 69

PRACTICE MASTER 70

Trace and write.

Z Z Z Z Z Z Z

Zelda gazed at the zebras.

Write a name that begins with Z.

Name

Copyright © Zaner-Bloser, Inc.   PRACTICE MASTER 70

ALPHABET ZOO CREATURES

Ask children to join in singing the popular Raffi song "Going to the Zoo." Invite them to help you create an alphabet zoo of letters turned into animal creatures. Give each child a 5" oak tag square. Assign letters and have children use a marker to write their letters. Then have them use pencils and crayons to turn the letters into new zoo creatures. Have children label their creatures and arrange them to create a zoo scene on a bulletin board. (visual, kinesthetic)

On guidelines on the chalkboard write **vV, yY, wW, xX, kK,** and **zZ.** Have children take turns naming the letter pairs and pointing to each uppercase and lowercase letter.

Call attention to the size and shape of letters by asking questions such as these: Which short letter goes below the baseline? Which letters look alike except for their size? Which letters have both slant right and slant left strokes?

MODEL

Write **vV** on guidelines as you say the stroke descriptions for each letter. Model writing the letters in the air as you repeat the descriptions. Have children echo them as they write the letters in the air with you. Follow the same procedure for **yY, wW, xX, kK,** and **zZ.**

PRACTICE

Let children practice writing the letter pairs **vV, yY, wW, xX, kK,** and **zZ** on laminated writing cards or slates before they write on the pages.

Review Write the letters.

vV yY wW xX kK zZ

Use the letters to write words.

wave   wax   joy   kit   fuzz

Write your name.

Circle your best word.

88

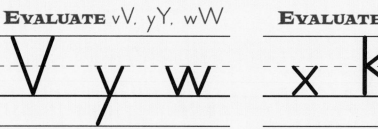

EVALUATE vV, yY, wW

V y w

To help children evaluate their writing, ask questions such as these:
Does your **v** touch the midline and baseline?
Do your **v** and **V** look alike except for size?
Does your **y** touch the headline of the next writing space?
Does your **w** have four slant strokes?
Is your **W** about the same width as the model?

EVALUATE xX, kK, zZ

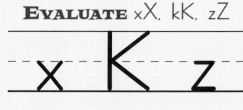

x K z

To help children evaluate their writing, ask questions such as these:
Do your **x** and **X** look alike except for size?
Does your **k** have two slant strokes?
Is your **K** about the same width as the model?
Do your **z** and **Z** look alike except for size?
Is your **Z** about the same width as the model?

88

Write the sentences.

Yoo-hoo.

Watch the birdie.

Keep your eyes open.

My Words

Put a 😊 next to your best sentence.

89

WRITE SENTENCES

Before children write the sentences on the page, review the importance of using guidelines to write letters. Have volunteers choose a letter from the page and tell where it begins and ends. Call attention to letters that go below the baseline. After children write, have them compare the placement and size of their letters with the models. Guide them to recognize why one sentence might be better than another.

MY WORDS

Ask children to write words of their own. Encourage them to write words that contain the review letters. If they need help, suggest they look for words on the previous pages.

COACHING HINT

Prepare tactile letters or sandpaper letters. Have children close their eyes, touch a letter, and identify it by its size and shape. You may need to guide a child's direction in exploring the letter shape. (kinesthetic)

STORYBOOK PHOTO ALBUM

Invite children to draw a picture of their favorite character from a storybook. Have them label their "photos" with a few words or a sentence. Put all the pictures into a large photo album and place it in the reading center. (visual)

MAKE US SMILE

Assign children to small groups. Provide each group with chart paper that has a border set aside for pictures. Invite children to work cooperatively to write sentences on the chart that tell what makes them smile. Then have them decorate the border of the chart with smiling faces cut from magazines. (visual)

Review with children that letters are used to make words, words can be put together to make sentences, and sentences can go together to create a story. Refer to the words on the page. Ask volunteers to read them aloud.

Tell children to write their own words or the words shown on the page. Provide materials for children to use as word sources.

PRACTICE

Let children practice writing words on laminated writing cards or slates before they write on the page.

Evaluation

Show What You Can Do

Here are words I can write.

_____

_____

_____

_____

_____

_____

_____

_____

_____

Write your name.

_____

_____

bus	play
run	map
van	hurry
kite	yellow
box	zoo

Circle your best word.

90

EVALUATE

To help children evaluate their writing, ask questions such as these:

Are all your letters straight up and down?
Are all the letters in your words correctly spaced?
Are your tall letters written between the headline and baseline?
Do your short letters begin at the midline or below it?
Do letters that go below the baseline touch the headline below?
Did you dot your **i** and **j**?

Encourage children to share their work with a peer and to have their partner circle the word he or she thinks is best.

Certificates of Progress *should be awarded to those children who show notable handwriting progress and Certificates of Excellence to those who progress to the top levels of handwriting proficiency.*

I can draw a picture.

I can write a story about my picture.

Put a 🙂 next to your best sentence.

STORY TIME

Display several picture books with interesting cover illustrations that show characters in action. Have children choose one to write about. Ask them to write about the characters shown and describe what is happening in the picture. Accept the use of invented spellings. After they write, ask them to read aloud their descriptions so their classmates can name the book being described. (visual)

PICTURE POSTCARDS

Give children manila drawing paper. On one side have them draw a picture of a place they have visited or would like to visit. Divide the other side to resemble a large postcard. Show children where to write a message and where to write the address. Then let children write their own postcard messages. Provide time for sharing. (visual)

WRITE SENTENCES

Before children write, encourage a lively sharing of ideas about the different subjects they might choose for their pictures and story writing. You might list their suggestions on the chalkboard.

Encourage children to use several sentences to tell about their pictures. Remind them to begin each sentence with an uppercase letter and to include an end mark. Point out that they may find it helpful to use some of the words they wrote on the previous page.

After they write, have children check the spacing between words and sentences. Guide them to see why one sentence might be better than another.

Ask children to share their pictures and stories.

COACHING HINT

Children's progress in handwriting is greater when instruction is given in short, intensive periods of approximately fifteen minutes daily. Now that children have been introduced to the formation of all the letters, this time can be used to promote an increasing ease with writing.

Dear Mom and Dad,
We are having fun here. I went swimming.
Love,
Peter

Mr. and Mrs. Cook
31 Tree St.
Forest, NY
12345

Write the following rhyme on chart paper and read it with the children, pointing to the words as you do.

One, two, buckle my shoe,
Three, four, shut the door,
Five, six, pick up sticks,
Seven, eight, lay them
    straight,
Nine, ten, a big fat hen.

Have children identify number words in the verse. Then count to ten in Spanish, pausing after each number to have children repeat it. Write the words on the chalkboard. Have children match Spanish words to English words in the rhyme.

Invite children to share other number rhymes they know in English, Spanish, and other languages.

92

Number Words Write the numerals and the number words.

1 one uno   2 two dos

3 three tres   4 four cuatro

5 five cinco

Circle your best word.

On Your Own Write the Spanish words for 2 and 5.

92

EVALUATE

O i e c u

To help children evaluate the size and shape of their short letters, ask questions such as these:
Do your short letters touch the midline and the baseline?
Does **o** begin below the midline?
Are the pull down straight strokes in your **a** and **i** straight?
Does your **e** begin with a slide right stroke?
Are your **o** and **c** round?
Does your **u** rest on the baseline?

Have children choose several words they have written on the page and evaluate their writing by comparing the size and shape of their letters with the models.

Practice Masters 91–109 provide practice in writing in Spanish.

Write the numerals and the number words.

6 six   seis   7 seven   siete

8 eight ocho   9 nine nueve

10 ten   diez

Circle your best word.

On Your Own Write a numeral and a number word to tell your age.

I see five fish.

NUMBER STORY BOOKLET

Invite children to create a booklet with an illustration and sentence about each number word in this lesson. Encourage them to include number words in Spanish and English in their sentences. Remind them to write sentences neatly with correct spacing between letters and words. Have them point out a word or sentence that is neatly written on a peer's paper. Bind the pages and share the pictures and stories with others. (visual)

EVALUATE

t h d

To help children evaluate the size and shape of their tall letters, ask questions such as these:
Do your tall letters touch the headline?
Do your tall letters rest on the baseline?
Are the pull down straight strokes in your **t** and **d** straight?
Is your **t** crossed at the midline?
Does your **h** begin at the headline?

Have children choose several words they have written on the page and evaluate their writing by comparing the size and shape of their letters with the models. Guide children to recognize why one word is better than another.

COACHING HINT

To help children write a backward circle, invite them to walk or hop in a counter-clockwise direction around a circle you have made on the floor with tape. Place a star to mark the beginning point of the circle. Then ask children to find letters with backward circles in the number words (**a, c, d, e, g, o**). On guidelines on the chalkboard, write circles between the midline and baseline. Have children take turns tracing all, or part, of each circle to help them form the letters **a, c, d, e, g,** and **o**. (kinesthetic)

JUST HOW MANY?

On chart paper, list the names of objects in your classroom, leaving a space before each word for a child to write a numeral and number word. For example, _____ *chairs.* Have each child choose a word, count the number of those items they see, and fill in the blank space. Read the chart together. (visual)

Write the chorus and first verse of "Here We Go 'Round the Mulberry Bush" on chart paper, underlining the day of the week. Prepare word cards, each printed with the name of a day of the week. Invite children to sing as you point to the words. Encourage children to make up new verses for each day of the week by adding phrases about things they do at school. Hold up the word card for the day as the children sing.

Chorus:

Here we go 'round
the mulberry bush,
the mulberry bush,
the mulberry bush.

Here we go 'round
the mulberry bush,
So early in the morning.

First Verse:

This is the way we
go to school,
go to school,
go to school,

This is the way
we go to school,
So early Monday morning.

Ask children what they notice about the first letter in the name of each day.

Days of the Week Write the name of each day.

Monday   Tuesday

Wednesday   Thursday

Friday   Saturday   Sunday

On Your Own What is today?

Circle your best word.

94

EVALUATE

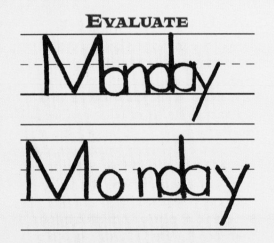

To help children evaluate the spacing between letters in a word, ask questions such as these:
Do any of your letters touch?
Are any of your letters too close together?
Are any of your letters too far apart?
Are your letters correctly spaced?

Dear _____ ,

Today is _____

_____

_____

_____

_____

Your friend,

_____

_____

95

EVALUATE

DearSue

Remind children that spaces between words in a sentence show readers where one word ends and the next begins.

To help children evaluate the spacing between words in a sentence, ask questions such as these:
Can you put an index finger between the word *Dear* and the name of your friend?
Can you put an index finger between the words *Today* and *is*?
Choose two words that are side by side. Can you put an index finger between them?
Is the space between your sentences wider than the space between words?

You may want children to work with partners. Ask them to read their letters to a partner and ask the partner to comment on the spacing of letters in words and words in sentences.

COACHING HINT

Make several sentence strips. Cut the words apart exactly where they begin and end. Place each cut up sentence in a plastic bag. Invite children, individually or in pairs, to arrange the words into sentences. Have them place their index fingers between words to determine correct spacing. Then invite children to write the sentence with correct spacing on the chalkboard. (kinesthetic)

DAILY DIARY

Staple together seven pieces of writing paper. Invite children to keep a diary for one week. Explain that they will write about the things they enjoyed doing on each day. To begin each page, have children write *Today is (day of the week)*. Provide time at the end of each day for children to write about the day. At the end of the week, invite children to read from their diaries. (visual)

Today is hot.

A WEATHER CHART

Have children record the weather each day for a week. Elicit words that describe weather, such as *sunny, cloudy, cold, hot, warm, windy,* and *rainy* and list them on a chart. To begin each daily record, have children write *Today is (_____)* and complete the sentence with words that describe the weather. (visual)

Write the following rhyme on chart paper, and underline *January.* Read it to children. Then have them read it with you as you point to the words.

Apples, peaches, pears, and plums,

Tell me when your birthday comes.

"January"—J-a-n-u-a-r-y

Repeat the verse substituting each month and have children stand when they hear their birthday month.

List the names of the months. Use tally marks to show how many children have birthdays in each month.

Months Write the name of each month.

January   February

March   April

May   June

Circle your best word.

On Your Own Write the name of your favorite month.

96

EVALUATE

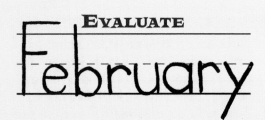

February

After children write, focus on the size of their letters. Ask them to compare their tall letters in each month's name with the models.

To help children evaluate the size of their letters, ask questions such as these:
Do your uppercase letters touch the headline?
Does your **y** go below the baseline and touch the next guideline?
Does your **p** go below the baseline and touch the next guideline?
Which tall letters did you write in *March?*

Suggest that children look at their word *February* and evaluate the size of the letters by comparing their word with the model.

Write the name of each month.

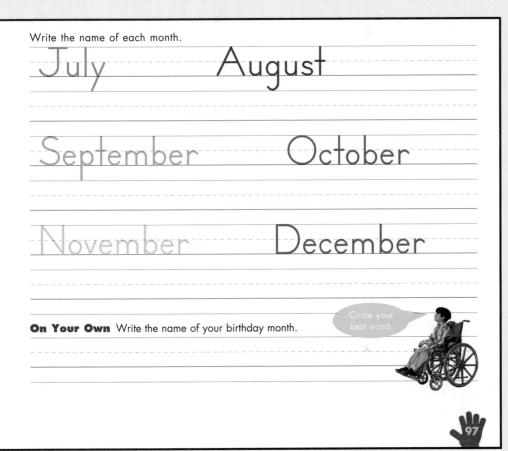

July   August

September   October

November   December

On Your Own Write the name of your birthday month.

Circle your best word.

97

EVALUATE

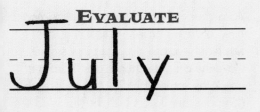

July

Remind children that using guidelines will help them write their letters the correct size.

To help children evaluate the size of their letters, ask questions such as these:
Do your uppercase letters touch the headline?
Does your **y** go below the baseline and touch the next guideline?
Does your **g** go below the baseline and touch the next guideline?
Does your **r** end below the midline?
Which tall letters did you write in *September*?

After children circle the month they think they wrote best, tell them to check that the letters are the correct size.

COACHING HINT

A left-handed child when writing at the chalkboard should stand a little to the right of his or her writing and pull the downstrokes toward the left elbow. The elbow is slightly bent, and the writing is done at a comfortable height on the chalkboard (between eyes and chin). As the writing progresses across the board, have the child move to the right to keep the downstrokes vertical. (kinesthetic)

WALL CALENDAR

Cut 12 nine-inch squares of drawing paper and of writing paper. Divide the class into twelve groups and assign each a month. Invite each group to design two squares for a wall calendar; one with an illustration depicting what usually happens in that month and the other with writing that describes it. Have children write the name of the month at the top of each paper, and arrange the squares to create a wall calendar. Have each group read aloud their sentences. (visual)

THIS MONTH

Talk about any special events or holidays that take place this month. Ask children to share ideas about what things they might like to do during the month. Have them write the name of the month at the top of a sheet of writing paper. Then ask them to write a list of things to do.

On chart paper, write this rhyme and ask children to listen for the color word as you read it aloud. Have one child underline each color word as you read the rhyme a second time.

Here's a box of crayons.
It's brand new.
Open it and find
Green, yellow, blue.

Look for orange, red,
And purple, too.
Six bright colors,
Just for you!

Write the words *rojo, amarillo, azul, verde, violeta,* and *naranja* on guidelines on the chalkboard. Name each color word in Spanish and have children repeat it after you. Match the English and Spanish words.

Next, name an object, such as an apple, the sun, the sky, or grass and ask children to name its color in both English and Spanish.

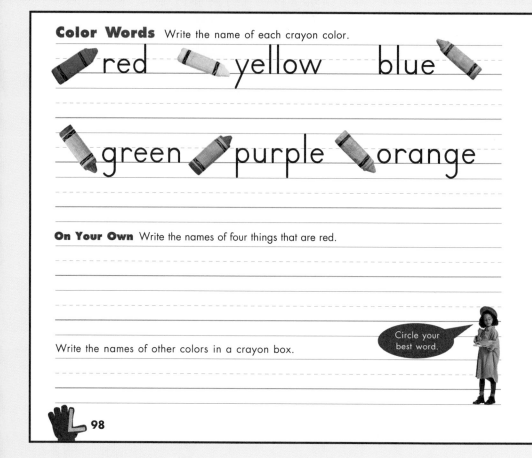

Color Words Write the name of each crayon color.

red   yellow   blue

green   purple   orange

On Your Own Write the names of four things that are red.

Write the names of other colors in a crayon box.

Circle your best word.

98

EVALUATE

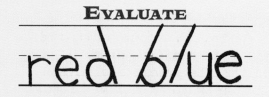

red blue

Remind children that manuscript letters are straight up and down.

To help children evaluate their writing, ask questions such as these:
Is your **d** straight up and down?
Is the pull down straight stroke in **b** straight?
Does your **l** touch the headline and the baseline?

As a check of good vertical quality, model how to draw parallel vertical lines over letters that have pull down straight strokes. Have the children choose one word and check the vertical quality. Ask children to compare their letters with the model to see if they are straight up and down.

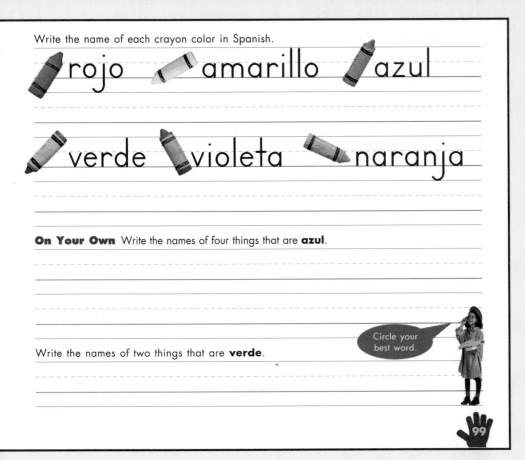

Write the name of each crayon color in Spanish.

rojo amarillo azul

verde violeta naranja

On Your Own Write the names of four things that are **azul**.

Write the names of two things that are **verde**.

Circle your best word.

99

EVALUATE

amarillo

To help children evaluate their writing, ask questions such as these:

Is your **d** straight up and down?

Does your **l** touch the headline and the baseline?

Does your **m** touch the baseline three times?

Have children choose one word in Spanish and check the vertical quality of their writing. Ask children to compare their letters with the model to see if they are straight up and down.

COACHING HINT

Practicing pull down straight strokes at the chalkboard is a good way to improve poor strokes, especially if these strokes tend to be slanted. Have the children use soft oversize chalk, holding it between the thumb and finger. You may want to begin by placing sets of two dots about six inches apart to mark the starting and stopping point of each vertical stroke. If children make the first stroke in a letter straight, the rest of the letter is more likely to be straight. (visual, kinesthetic)

Write Away

COLOR POEMS

Read some of the color poems in *Hailstones and Halibut Bones* by Mary O'Neill. Then invite children to write their own color poems. Suggest they name and describe things of that color or tell how the color makes them feel. Mount each poem on matching colored construction paper. Have children share their poems with classmates. (visual)

I don't like green. It makes me feel mean.

COLOR DESCRIPTIONS

Pair children. Have them write sentences, using color words to describe what their partner is wearing that day. Ask children to read their descriptions and let the class guess who is being described. (auditory, visual)

RAINBOWS

Have children draw or paint a rainbow and label each color with its name. (visual)

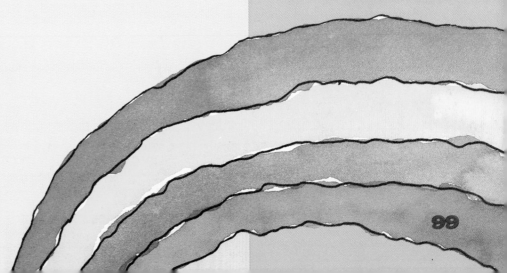

Write these Mother Goose rhymes on chart paper. Read them aloud and have children repeat them. Ask children which words rhyme, and have children underline the letters that are alike in each rhyming pair.

Jack be nimble, Jack be quick,
Jack jump over the candlestick.

Rain, rain, go away,
Come again another day.
Little Johnny wants to play.

Wee Willie Winkie runs through the town,
Upstairs and downstairs, in his nightgown;
Rapping at the window, crying through the lock,
"Are the children in their beds?
Now it's eight o'clock."

Invite children to name rhyming words or recite other familiar rhymes.

100

Rhyming Words Write the words.

bee   see   tree

sat   cat   hat

fly   try   by

On Your Own Write words that rhyme with **all**.

Circle your best word.

100

EVALUATE

bee

b e e

Remind children that letters in a word that are close or too far apart are hard to read.

To help them evaluate the spacing between letters in a word, ask questions such as these:
Are any of your letters too far apart?
Do any of your letters touch?

Invite children to do some reciprocal teaching. Have one child write two words on the chalkboard, one with letters spaced correctly and the other with letters spaced too far apart. Then have the child choose a classmate to circle the word that is correctly written. Repeat several times.

Write each rhyme.

Did the fly go by?

Is a cat in the hat?

Is a bee in the tree?

On Your Own Write words that rhyme.

Put a ☺ next to your best sentence.

A BOOK OF RHYMES

Invite children to create an original two-line rhyme and draw a picture to illustrate it. They may also enjoy copying a favorite rhyme or poem on writing paper and illustrating it. Collect all the completed rhymes and put them together to make a book. (auditory, visual)

EVALUATE

flygo

Remind children that spaces between words in a sentence show readers where one word ends and the next begins.

To help children evaluate the spacing, ask questions such as these:
Did you leave about the same space between words?
Is your spacing between words about the width of your index finger?
Choose two words. Can you put an index finger between them?
Is the space between your sentences wider than the space between words?

COACHING HINT

To reinforce manuscript writing throughout the year, have children do many different kinds of writing. Activities may include the following:
Label pictures and objects.
Make lists of things in categories.
Write invitations.
Write about field trips.
Write facts.
Retell a story in writing.
Write about books.
Write stories, poems, and descriptions.

When children practice the writing skills they have learned in practical ways, they come to see the importance of writing.

RHYMING WORD CARDS

Have children illustrate pairs of rhyming words on separate cards. Direct them to draw a picture on one side of the card and to write the word for the picture on the other side. Children will discover the rhyming words by naming the pictures or by reading the words in each pair. (auditory, visual)

Write the following song on chart paper, underlining the contraction *I'm*. Invite children to sing with you.

I'm a little teapot,
Short and stout.
Here is my handle.
Here is my spout.

When I get all
steamed up,
Hear me shout,
"Tip me over
And pour me out."

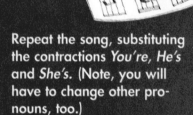

Repeat the song, substituting the contractions *You're, He's* and *She's*. (Note, you will have to change other pronouns, too.)

Ask children to tell what two words each contraction stands for.

Point out that the apostrophe begins just below the headline.

Contractions Write the words with an ' . Then write the sentences.

I'm

I am seven.

I'm seven.

you're

You are six.

You're six.

On Your Own Write a sentence about yourself. Begin with **I'm.**

Circle your best word.

102

EVALUATE

I'm

Remind children that using guidelines will help them write letters the correct size.

To help them evaluate their writing, ask questions such as these:

Do your uppercase letters begin at the headline?

Does your **e** rest on the baseline?

Does your **I** have a slide right at the headline and another at the baseline?

Does your apostrophe begin just below the headline?

Have children find a partner's best sentence. If any letters are not written within the guidelines, suggest they point this out.

Write the words with an **'**. Then write the sentences.

he's

she's

He is nine.

She is ten.

He's nine.

She's ten.

On Your Own Write a sentence about a friend.

Put a ☺ next to your best sentence.

103

EVALUATE

She 's

To help children evaluate the size of their letters, ask questions such as these:
Do your tall letters touch the headline?
Does your **e** rest on the baseline?
Does your **S** begin below the headline and end above the baseline?
Does your apostrophe touch the headline?

COACHING HINT

Show children how to use a ruler to draw horizontal lines along the tops of letters to show correct size. Have children use this technique to evaluate the size of their letters. (visual)

To review pull down straight strokes and retraces, make vertical lines with tape or chalk. Ask children to walk the line, placing one foot in front of the other. Tell them to turn and walk back over the same line to reinforce the concept of retracing. Have them name the letters that include a retrace. (kinesthetic)

ALL ABOUT FEELINGS

Write the following sentence starters on guidelines on the chalkboard:

I'm happy when _____.
You're sad when _____.
He's angry when _____.
She's surprised when _____.

Ask children to find the contractions in each sentence. Invite them to write each sentence starter and complete with their own ideas. (visual)

PUT IT TOGETHER

Review the four contractions on the pages. Then have children brainstorm a list of other contractions they use. To stimulate their thinking, you might write the following words on the board: *do not, can not, will not, he will, she will, I will.* (auditory, visual)

She is surprised when it's her birthday.

Invite children to sing "Head, Shoulders, Knees, and Toes."

Head, shoulders, knees, and toes,
Knees, and toes.
Head, shoulders, knees, and toes,
Knees, and toes.
Eyes, ears, mouth, and nose.
Head, shoulders, knees, and toes,
Knees, and toes.

Have children name and point to the body parts mentioned in the song.

Plurals Write the word. Then write the word that shows more than one.

One	More Than One
eye	eyes
ear	ears
shoulder	shoulders

On Your Own Write other words that show more than one.

Circle your best word.

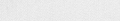

104

EVALUATE

ear

To help children evaluate the size and shape of their letters, ask questions such as these:

Is your **e** round?
Are your curves in **s** about the same size?
Did you begin **h** with a pull down straight stroke?
Did you begin **r** with a pull down straight stroke?
Does your **a** begin with a backward circle?
Which other letters are formed with backward circles?

Have children choose a word and compare its size and shape to the model.

Write the word. Then write the word that shows more than one.

One	More Than One
elbow	elbows
wrist	wrists
knee	knees

On Your Own Write other words that show more than one.

Circle your best word.

lions

COUNT THE ANIMALS

Write some animal names on the chalkboard. Choose only names whose plurals are formed by adding **s**. Invite children to choose an animal, write its name on lined paper, and add an **s** to indicate more than one. Attach the paper to drawing paper and have children illustrate the word by drawing two or more of the same animals. Then have them write a number word to show how many and cover it with a flap. Finally, have them exchange papers, count the animals, and check their answer by lifting the flap. Keep the animal counting pictures for other math activities. (visual)

LABEL BODY PARTS

Ask children to draw a person or animal and label the parts of the body. Invite them to share their drawings. (visual)

EVALUATE

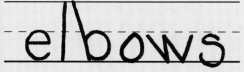

To help children evaluate the size and shape of their letters, ask questions such as these:
Is your **o** round?
Are your curves in **s** about the same size?
Did you begin **b** with a pull down straight stroke?
Did you begin **n** with a pull down straight stroke?
Does your **w** have four slant strokes?
Does your **k** have two slant strokes?

COACHING HINT

Using correct body position when writing will help children write better letters. They will also not tire as quickly. Encourage them to sit comfortably erect with their feet flat on the floor and their hips touching the back of the chair. Both arms should rest on the desk with the elbows off the desk. Be sure children are relaxed, holding their pencils correctly.

Invite children to say hello in these languages

French: *bonjour*
Spanish: *hola*
Swahili: *jambo*

Print the following rhyme on chart paper and read it with the children.

One misty moisty morning,
When cloudy was the day,
I chanced to meet an old friend
Walking on her way.
She began to smile
And I began to grin.
How do you do, and how do you do,
And how do you do again?

Frame the words *how do you do* and explain that this phrase is a way of saying *hello*. Reread the poem, substituting *hello* for *how do you do* in several languages.

Say the words for *good-bye* and have children echo you.

Spanish: *adios*
Italian: *ciao*
Hebrew: *shalom*

106

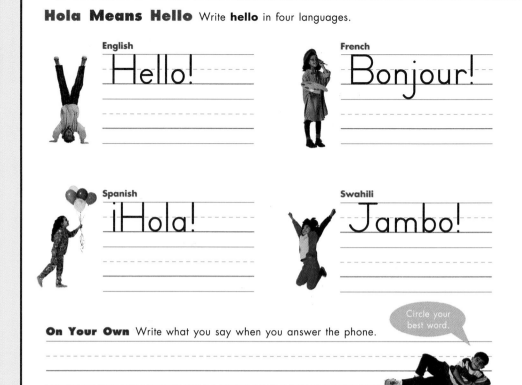

Hola Means Hello Write **hello** in four languages.

English
Hello!

French
Bonjour!

Spanish
¡Hola!

Swahili
Jambo!

Circle your best word.

On Your Own Write what you say when you answer the phone.

106

EVALUATE

Review with children that manuscript letters are straight up and down.

To help children evaluate their writing, ask questions such as these:
Is your **b** straight up and down?
Is the pull down straight stroke in **l** straight?
Does your **H** touch the headline and the baseline?
Does your **m** stand up straight?

Jambo

Review how to draw parallel vertical lines over pull down straight strokes to check for vertical quality. Ask children to compare their letters with the model to see if they are straight up and down.

Write **good-bye** in four languages.

English
Good-bye!

Hebrew
Shalom!

Italian
Ciao!

Spanish
¡Adiós!

Circle your best word.

On Your Own Write what you say as you leave a friend.

107

Hello Mom,
Thank you for the
scarf I wear when
it's cold outside.
Good-bye

THANK-YOU NOTE

Ask children to write a thank-you note on lined paper to someone who has given them a gift. They may want to begin their greeting using *hello* and end it with *good-bye.* Suggest they tell why they like the gift or how they are using it. Encourage children to give or send the note. (visual)

CREATIVE WRITING

Invite children to write a real or make-believe story about two people or two animals meeting for the first time. Suggest they include the word *hello* in any language as part of their stories. Do not discourage the use of invented spelling. Remind children to use correct spacing between words. Provide time for children to share their stories with classmates. (visual)

EVALUATE

To help children evaluate their writing, ask questions such as these:
Is your **d** straight up and down?
Is the pull down straight stroke in **b** straight?
Does your **l** touch the headline and the baseline?
Is your exclamation point straight?
Does your **h** have a retrace?

Remind children that writing a word correctly requires them to think about a letter's size and shape.

COACHING HINT

Make children aware of their improvement in handwriting. Help them compare samples of their writing from the beginning of the year with their present work. This will provide motivation for further progress, particularly for children who have had difficulties.

Invite children to share their
thoughts about what they
have accomplished in handwriting. Help them discuss
their progress in writing letters with correct size, shape,
and spacing.

Explain that they will show
what they can do by writing
their own letters, words,
and sentences. You may
wish to provide materials
for children to use as
sources.

PRACTICE

Let children practice writing
words on laminated writing
cards or slates before they
write on the page.

Posttest
Show What You Can Do

Here are letters I can write.

Here are words I can write.

Here are names I can write.

Circle your
best word

Write your name.

108

EVALUATE

To help children evaluate their writing, ask
questions such as these:

Are all your letters straight up and down?
Are your letters with circles round?
Do letters that go below the baseline touch
the headline below?
Did you dot your **i** and **j** and cross your **t**?
Did you use an uppercase letter to begin
each name?
Do all your uppercase letters touch the
headline and baseline?

Certificates of Progress *should be awarded
to those children who show notable handwriting progress and* Certificates of
Excellence *to those who progress to the top
levels of handwriting proficiency.*

Write a story of your own.

_____

Put a ☺ next to your best sentence.

109

Invite children to contribute ideas to a list of topics they would enjoy writing about. Have children write three suggestions and organize their ideas on chart paper. Display the chart in the writing center. When they have free time, encourage them to write about and illustrate one of the topics.
(visual)

On Summer vacation we went camping.

ON AND ON STORIES

Have children work in small groups to write a story. Suggest they decide on a topic and choose one group member to start the story by writing a sentence. Then ask members to take turns continuing the story by saying a sentence and writing it. Encourage them to share their completed stories.
(auditory)

WRITE SENTENCES

Before children write, encourage a lively sharing of ideas about the different subjects they might choose for their story writing. Suggest they begin by writing a title.

Remind them to begin each sentence with an uppercase letter and to include an end mark. Accept the use of invented spellings.

After they write, have children check the spacing between words and sentences. Guide children to see why one sentence might be better than another.

Some children may wish to share their pictures and stories with their classmates.

HANDWRITING AND THE WRITING PROCESS

If you use a writing process in your class, have children follow it to complete the page. The steps might include

Prewriting
What should I write about?
Drafting
I write my ideas in sentences.
Revising
What should I change?
Editing
How can I improve my handwriting and spelling?
Publishing
How will I share my work?

As children participate in the writing process, let them know that good handwriting is always important. Notes, webs, story drafts, and published pieces that are easy to read cut down on confusion in your classroom and help children express their ideas clearly and confidently.

The Record of Student's Handwriting Skills serves to indicate each student's progress in mastering the skills presented. The chart lists the essential skills in the program. After the skills that are listed have been practiced and evaluated, you will be able to mark the Record of Student's Handwriting Skills for either *Shows Mastery or Needs Improvement.*

Record of Student's Handwriting Skills

Manuscript

	Needs Improvement	Shows Mastery		Needs Improvement	Shows Mastery
Positions paper correctly	☐	☐	Writes **e** and **E**	☐	☐
Holds pencil correctly	☐	☐	Writes **f** and **F**	☐	☐
Writes stand up straight lines	☐	☐	Writes **g** and **G**	☐	☐
Writes lie down straight lines	☐	☐	Writes **j** and **J**	☐	☐
Writes backward circles	☐	☐	Writes **q** and **Q**	☐	☐
Writes forward circles	☐	☐	Writes **u** and **U**	☐	☐
Writes slant lines	☐	☐	Writes **s** and **S**	☐	☐
Writes four kinds of lines	☐	☐	Writes **b** and **B**	☐	☐
Writes numerals **1–5**	☐	☐	Writes **p** and **P**	☐	☐
Writes numerals **6–10**	☐	☐	Writes **r** and **R**	☐	☐
Writes **l** and **L**	☐	☐	Writes **n** and **N**	☐	☐
Writes **i** and **I**	☐	☐	Writes **m** and **M**	☐	☐
Writes **t** and **T**	☐	☐	Writes **h** and **H**	☐	☐
Writes **o** and **O**	☐	☐	Writes **v** and **V**	☐	☐
Writes **a** and **A**	☐	☐	Writes **y** and **Y**	☐	☐
Writes **d** and **D**	☐	☐	Writes **w** and **W**	☐	☐
Writes an exclamation point	☐	☐	Writes **x** and **X**	☐	☐
Writes a question mark	☐	☐	Writes **k** and **K**	☐	☐
Writes **c** and **C**	☐	☐	Writes **z** and **Z**	☐	☐

110

SHOWS MASTERY

Mastery of written letterforms is achieved when the student writes the letters using correct basic strokes. Compare the student's written letterforms with the letter models shown in the book. Keep in mind the keys to legibility (size and shape, slant, and spacing) when evaluating letters, numerals, punctuation marks, words, and sentences for mastery of skill. Observation will indicate whether a student has mastered such skills as pencil and paper positions.

Check the appropriate box for each skill.

NEEDS IMPROVEMENT

If a student has not mastered a skill, provide additional basic instruction and practice. First, determine the student's specific needs. Then return to the initial teaching steps of the lesson for ways to help the student. To improve letterforms, have the student practice writing the letter in isolation and within words and sentences. Reinforce instruction through activities geared to the student's modality strengths. Ask the student to evaluate his or her writing with you. Reevaluate the student's writing following practice over time. When mastery of the skill is achieved, check *Shows Mastery.*

The Record of Student's Handwriting Skills is reproduced on Practice Master 71.

Index

Alphabet
  book, 113–120
  chart, 12–13
Book, making a, 112
Color words, writing, 98–99
Contractions, writing, 102–103
Days of the week, writing, 94–95
Evaluation, 54–55, 90–91
  posttest, 108–109
  pretest, 6–7
  record of student's handwriting skills, 110
  self-evaluation, 20, 21, 22, 23, 24, 25, 26, 27, 28, 29, 30, 31, 32,
    33, 34, 35, 36, 37, 38, 39, 40, 41, 42, 43, 44, 45, 46, 47, 48,
    49, 50, 51, 52, 53, 54, 55, 56, 57, 58, 59, 60, 61, 62, 63, 64, 65,
    66, 67, 68, 69, 70, 71, 72, 73, 74, 75, 76, 77, 78, 79, 80, 81, 82,
    83, 84, 85, 86, 87, 88, 89, 90, 91, 92, 93, 94, 96, 97, 98, 99,
    100, 101, 102, 103, 104, 105, 106, 107, 108, 109
Guidelines, using, 10–11
Left-handed writers, 8
*Legibility, Keys to, 10–11
Letter groupings
  lL, iI, tT, oO, aA, dD, 24–35, 38–39
  cC, eE, fF, gG, jJ, qQ, 40–53
  uU, sS, bB, pP, 56–65
  rR, nN, mM, hH, 66–75
  vV, yY, wW, xX, kK, zZ, 76–89
Letters
  lowercase, 12–13
  a, 32–33; b, 60–61; c, 40–41; d, 34–35; e, 42–43; f, 44–45;
  g, 46–47; h, 72–73; i, 26–27; j, 48–49; k, 84–85; l, 24–25;
  m, 70–71; n, 68–69; o, 30–31; p, 62–63; q, 50–51; r, 66–67;
  s, 58–59; t, 28–29; u, 56–57; v, 76–77; w, 80–81; x, 82–83;
  y, 78–79; z, 86–87
  uppercase, 12–13
  A, 32–33; B, 60–61; C, 40–41; D, 34–35; E, 42–43; F, 44–45;
  G, 46–47; H, 72–73; I, 26–27; J, 48–49; K, 84–85; L, 24–25;
  M, 70–71; N, 68–69; O, 30–31; P, 62–63; Q, 50–51; R, 66–67;
  S, 58–59; T, 28–29; U, 56–57; V, 76–77; W, 80–81; X, 82–83;
  Y, 78–79; Z, 86–87
Lines
  backward circles, 16, 19
  forward circles, 17, 19
  lie down straight, 15, 19
  slant, 18, 19
  stand up straight, 14, 19
Months, writing, 96–97
Number words, writing, 92–93
Numerals, 13
  writing 1–5, 20–21
  writing 6–10, 22–23
Plurals, writing, 104–105
Positions
  paper, 8–9
  pencil, 8–9
  sitting, 8–9
Posttest, 108–109
Pretest, 6–7
Prewriting, 5–19
Punctuation marks
  apostrophe, 102–103
  exclamation point, 36–37
  question mark, 36–37
Record of student's handwriting skills, 110
Review, 38–39, 52–53, 64–65, 74–75, 88–89
Rhyming words, writing, 100–101
Right-handed writers, 9
Writing applications
  book, 113–120
  friendly letter, 95
  story, 55, 91, 109
Writing extensions
  25, 27, 29, 31, 33, 35, 37, 39, 41, 43, 45, 47, 49, 51, 53, 57, 59,
  61, 63, 65, 67, 69, 71, 73, 75, 77, 79, 81, 83, 85, 87, 89, 92, 93,
  94, 96, 97, 98, 99, 101, 102, 103, 104, 105, 106, 107
Writing in other languages
  French, 106
  Hebrew, 107
  Italian, 107
  Spanish, 92–93, 99, 106–107
  Swahili, 106

***Keys to Legibility, including size and shape, slant, and
spacing, are implicitly covered in each student lesson and
are explicitly dealt with in the Teacher Edition. These
terms are introduced in Grade 2.**

III

Make a Book

After you take pages out of this book, you can make a little ABC book.

1. Cut along the dashed line.

3. Cut along the dashed line.

5. Cut along the dashed line.

7. Cut along the dashed line.

2. Place the x-ray fish on top of the zebra. Now you have started a pile.

4. Place the tiger on top of the vulture. Add these pages to the top of your pile.

6. Place the panda on top of the reindeer. Add these pages to the top of your pile.

8. Place the lion on top of the newt. Add these pages to the top of your pile.

9. Now start folding. Fold over on the middle line, one page at a time.

10. Turn the book over to see Animals A to Z.

Children will enjoy reading and writing their very own ABC book. You may decide to have them write the letters and words in alphabetical order after you staple the books together. Or you might send the books to be completed at home by the children with their family. The facts that follow may be helpful to you as you discuss the ABC animals in the children's book.

Zz

zebra

31

Write 1–5.

I caught a fish alive.

4

Xx

x-ray fish

29

Zebra

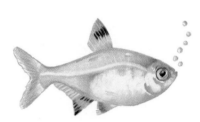

X-ray Fish

Zebra

Two types of zebra live in the central and southern parts of Africa. A limited population of small zebras lives in the hills, but a vast number of large zebras live on the African plains. Zebras are vegetarians and live on a variety of grasses. They migrate over large distances for food and water. Large zebras are best known for their black and white stripes. They closely resemble horses in size, shape, and features. Family groups travel in large communities. The zebra's enemies are lions and hyenas.

X-ray fish

X-ray fish live in South America in warm water. They eat worms, insects, and small crustaceans. The x-ray fish got its name because its body is translucent. Some of its internal organs are visible. The fish is a silvery color, with wide, black stripes on its fins. It is small, less than two inches long.

113

Yak

Yak

Wild yaks live in the hills and mountains of Tibet and central Asia. They spend the winter in the lowlands and the summer in the higher mountains. Yaks are vegetarians, eating grasses, leaves of bushes, and small twigs. The wild yak has long, black hair over its body and a large, bushy tail. Tame, smaller yaks have brown-black coats. Most wild yaks travel in large herds, but males generally stay alone. Trained yaks are used for travel and work. Milk from these yaks is used for food. Yaks make grunting sounds and are sometimes called "grunting oxen."

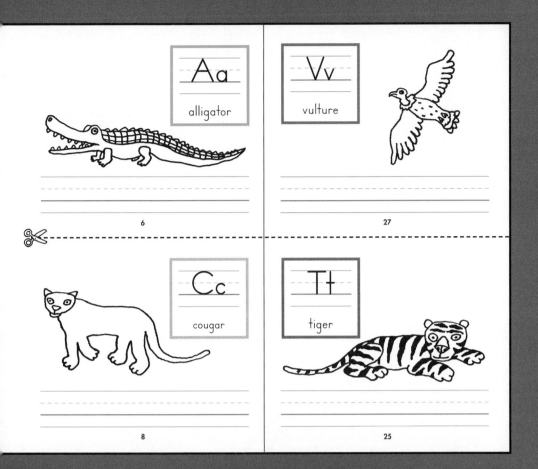

Aa alligator

6

Vv vulture

27

Cc cougar

8

Tt tiger

25

Alligator

Cougar

Vulture

Tiger

Alligator

Alligators live along the edges of lakes, swamps, and rivers in the southeastern United States. They usually eat fish and small animals. Alligators look like large lizards. Their eyes, ears, and nose can be above the water while the rest of them is underwater. They have long, powerful tails. They lay 20–70 eggs in a large mud nest. Before they hatch, the babies make sounds that call the mother. Alligators hiss. Males roar very loudly.

Cougar

Cougars live in forests and grasslands of North America. Their diet consists of rodents, small animals, and deer. Cougars have slender bodies with brown coats and use their black-tipped tails for balance. Their sensitive ears are small and pointy. They can purr and hiss but are generally quiet. Cougars are also called *pumas* and *mountain lions*. They hunt over a large range but stay away from other cougars.

Vulture

There are several types of vulture. Vultures are found in Africa, southern Asia, the southern United States, and South America. They are scavengers and eat only dead animals. Some types have gaudily colored necks, bald heads, and hooked beaks, and their feathers are usually dark brown or black. Most have broad wings. They are powerful, skilled flyers. They plunge down quickly, yet make a soft landing. Vultures make raucous squawking sounds when feeding.

Tiger

The tiger's habitats in China, India, and Indonesia are very limited. Tigers hunt and eat large animals. The tiger is the largest of the cat family. Most have black stripes on an orange-brown coat and a white underside. Some types have a white coat with black stripes. Tigers tend to be solitary. They frequently drink when eating. There are just a few thousand tigers left, making them an endangered species. Tigers roar loudly and also grunt and growl.

Walrus

Umbrella Bird

Bear

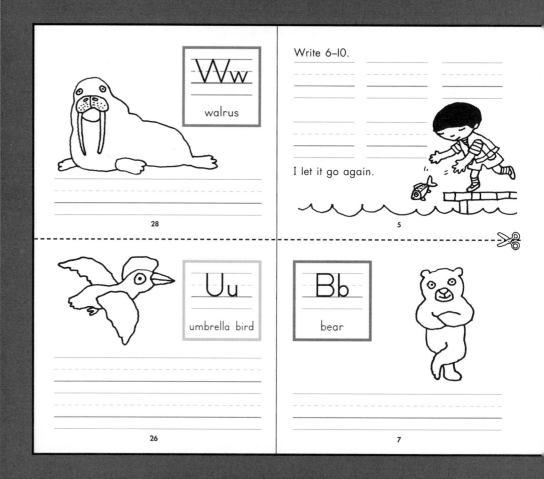

Walrus

Walruses live in coastal regions of the Arctic, North Atlantic, and North Pacific oceans. They feed on the ocean bottom for clams, crabs, worms, snails, shrimp, and starfish. A walrus is a heavy mammal, about 10 feet long, with small eyes, no external ears, long tusks, and flipper-like limbs. Walruses use their tusks to dig for food and also to help them climb onto rocks or ice floes. Walruses gather in large herds and mostly sleep when on land. Polar bears and humans are their enemies. A walrus makes a low-pitched ringing sound and, when excited, a loud, repeated roar.

Umbrella Bird

The umbrella bird is found in South America. The male umbrella bird has an unusual booming call. When he sends out his call, he changes his appearance. He puts on a show of color by inflating loose red skin on his breast, making the area look like a bright tomato. He also spreads his crest of feathers so that they form an umbrella-like canopy over his eyes and part of his beak.

Bear

Brown bears live in the colder climates of North America, Europe, and Siberia. They eat vegetation, berries, fish, and small rodents. They love honey and sweets. Bears have furry coats, powerful limbs, large claws, and an excellent sense of smell. Bears walk on all four legs but can stand on two. They hibernate during the winter. They make few sounds, chiefly grunts.

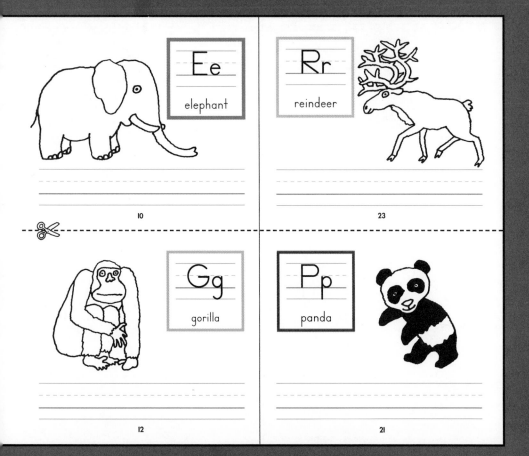

E e
elephant

10

R r
reindeer

23

G g
gorilla

12

P p
panda

21

Elephant

Gorilla

Elephant

Elephants are found in the grasslands of Africa and the forests of the Asian subcontinent. They feed on grasses, roots, tree bark, and fruit. The Asian elephant also eats bamboo. Elephants are the largest land animals, weighing up to 13,000 pounds. Their skin is gray-black. They use their trunks to collect food and water. They not only drink the water, they squirt it on their backs. They use their tusks to dig and their large ears to help cool their bodies. Elephants make a low-pitched growl and grunt. When excited, they scream and trumpet.

Gorilla

Gorillas live in family groups in the rain forests of central Africa. Gorillas are vegetarians. They eat leaves, fruits, flowers, and small branches. Adult males can be about 6 feet tall. They weigh about 400 pounds and have long arms. Some have black, shiny coats; some are silverbacks. Gorillas can grunt and make screaming sounds. Males sometimes beat their chests with their arms. Young gorillas can swing on tree branches; older ones stay on the ground.

Reindeer

Reindeer inhabit the subarctic and arctic regions of Asia and Europe. They are vegetarians and eat grasses, plants, and leaves of bushes. Reindeer can dig through snow and ice to find food. Males have larger antlers than females. The antlers are shed and grow anew every year. Reindeer have long legs, short tails, and a brown coat with a gray underside. Large herds migrate north in the summer and to southern woodlands in the winter. Tame reindeer provide milk for cheese and butter.

Reindeer

Panda

Giant pandas live in the Himalaya Mountains in China. Their main food is bamboo, but they will also eat wild fruits, mice, and insects. A panda looks like a bear with a white face, small black ears, and black areas around the eyes. Pandas are rare and endangered animals that live alone in the wild. They sit upright when eating. They can make a loud whinnying sound.

Panda

Seal

Quail

Dolphin

Fox

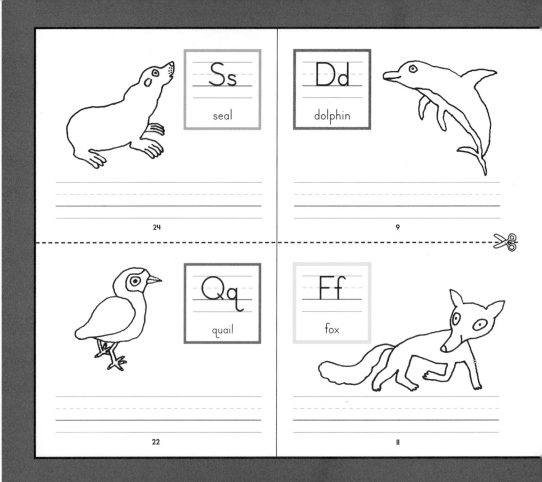

Ss
seal
24

Dd
dolphin
9

Qq
quail
22

Ff
fox
11

Seal

Seals are prevalent in polar regions and some temperate coastal waters. They eat mostly fish and krill, and some squid. Seals are mammals with a streamlined body, dense fur, and side and back flippers. Their color can be gray or brown. Some baby seals are white. There are about thirty types of seal. They are graceful, agile swimmers. Many can stay underwater for long periods. Seals breed on land, but feed in the water. They shed their fur. Seals make honking-like sounds. Some make clicks under water.

Quail

Quail live in Europe, Asia, and North America. They eat insects and seeds. The feathers of many types of quail are reddish-brown with streaks of white. The head is usually dark brown. Typical sounds and calls are of three notes. In North America one quail call sounds like "Bob White," and that is what the bird is named. Quail can lay more than ten eggs at a time. They gather in very large numbers when they migrate.

Dolphin

Many dolphin species are found in oceans, seas, and coastal waters in tropical and temperate climates. They feed on many types of fish, squid, and octopuses. Dolphins grow to between 6 and 10 feet and weigh up to 1,200 pounds. As air-breathing mammals, they have a blowhole on top of their heads. They communicate with intense, high-pitched clicking sounds and whistles and use echoes to locate food. Dolphins are fast swimmers and travel in groups. Babies ride on the mother's back.

Fox

Foxes live in forests on all the continents except Australia. Foxes eat mostly meat with a diet of small animals, fish, birds, insects, fruits, and nuts. A fox has the features of a dog, a pointy and sensitive nose, large ears, a reddish coat of fur, and a long, bushy tail. Foxes live alone or in a small family group. There are four to eight in a litter. Territories can extend to thousands of acres. Fox sounds range from soft barking between family members to loud yapping and howls.

Ii
iguana
14

Nn
newt
19

Kk
kangaroo
16

Ll
lion
17

Iguana

Kangaroo

Newt

Lion

Iguana

These lizards are found in several habitats: rain forests of Central and South America and the deserts of Mexico and the southwestern United States. An iguana's diet consists of insects and plants. The common iguana has a green body and a line of scales down its back. It can be as long as 6 feet from tip to tail. Iguanas are slow-moving lizards but good swimmers. The forest iguana is a skilled tree climber.

Kangaroo

All 50 kinds of kangaroos are found in Australia, New Zealand, and New Guinea. Some types live in grasslands and others in forests or rocky areas. Most kangaroos eat plants and grasses. Adult red and gray kangaroos are as big as an average person. They have a long, muscular tail, powerful hind legs, and short arms. They use their tails for balance. Large kangaroos are able to jump up to about 5 feet, and forward to about 20 feet. Babies are raised in their mother's pouch.

Newt

Newts are small salamanders that live in damp woodlands near water. The red-spotted newt is found in the United States. Their diet consists of insects and worms. The newt's slender body is less than five inches long. Its long tail is about the same size as its body. Newts hatch from eggs on underwater leaves. After birth, they live in the water and breathe through gills. Later they develop lungs and live on land. Finally they return to live in the water. Newts can grow a new leg if one is lost. They also shed their skin.

Lion

Lions are found on the sandy plains and grasslands of Africa. They hunt large animals such as zebras, buffaloes, and antelopes. Males have a massive head surrounded by a large mane. Females are smaller and have no mane. Lions' tails end in a tuft of black hair. Lion families are called *prides*. Cubs are playful, even with adults. Females are the main hunters and are active at night and in teams. Lions' roars are deep and loud. They also grunt, growl, and snarl.

Octopus

Monkey

Hippo

Jaguar

| Oo |
| octopus |

20

| Hh |
| hippo |

13

| Mm |
| monkey |

18

| Jj |
| jaguar |

15

Octopus

The octopus is found in the warm waters of the Caribbean and Mediterranean seas. Octopuses eat shellfish, crabs, lobsters, and clams. The octopus has eight tentacles each with hundreds of suckers. It takes on the color of its surroundings. It can change colors when disturbed. There are about 50 types of octopus, ranging in size from a few inches to about 25 feet. Octopuses can grow a new tentacle if one is lost. They move by expelling water from their head, and can squirt "ink" to escape danger. They can live in holes and cracks.

Monkey

Monkeys live in the forests and grasslands of Africa, South America, and Southern Asia. They eat fruits, leaves, nuts, and insects. Monkeys come in many sizes and colors: black, brown, gray, red, and white. All have tails. There are over one hundred kinds of monkey. They have dexterity in their hands and feet. Their tails are useful for swinging, climbing, and jumping. Monkeys live in groups. Howls, chirps, screeches, and barks are the sounds they make.

Hippo

Large hippos live in rivers and lakes in Africa. Pygmy hippos live in forests and swamps. They are vegetarians and eat grasses and underwater plants. Hippos have a long, stubby body, short legs, and a big head with tiny ears. They can weigh up to 3,000 pounds. Many large hippos live in groups of about 30 animals. They stay in water during the day and move onto land at night. Birds sometimes rest on the hippos' heads to look for food. Rapidly repeated deep grunts are the usual sounds hippos make.

Jaguar

Jaguars live in rain forests, wetlands, and grasslands. They range from South America up to Mexico. They eat large and small animals that they catch. A large member of the cat family, a jaguar can be over 6 feet long and weigh up to 200 pounds. Jaguars are good swimmers and can also climb trees. They move over large distances within their territories but live alone. They make a deep, hoarse grumble.